Do You Wanna Dance?

A Double Life

Deborah M. Porter

author**HOUSE**®

AuthorHouse™
1663 Liberty Drive, Suite 200
Bloomington, IN 47403
www.authorhouse.com
Phone: 1-800-839-8640

First published by AuthorHouse 10/27/2008

ISBN: 978-1-4389-2363-5 (sc)
ISBN: 978-1-4389-2362-8 (hc)

Printed in the United States of America
Bloomington, Indiana

This book is printed on acid-free paper.

Prologue

It was 1989, and Desiree Peters was foot loose and fancy free at the age of thirty- three. Getting married as a teenager, believing she knew it all; she quit high school and was married. Her groom was Timothy Andrews. He was a blonde haired, blue eyed; James Dean type. All of the girls wanted him, how lucky; she got him. The odds were stacked against them, and their marriage was doomed from the beginning. Their age and upbringing had not provided them with the tools they needed to have a successful marriage.

Together they had two sons, Jason and Jett. There was the house, the two children, the cars and the dog; no white picket fence, however. There was physical, and emotional abuse, Desiree had decided long ago; their marriage was over.

Without an education and no employment, she had a long road to travel. Desiree made the best of a bad situation for a long time. She was far from perfect. She had come from a dysfunctional family, and had no clue how to be married; however, she was a room mom, a soccer coach and loved her children.

Desiree was beginning to discover who she was. Stubborn and independent were adjectives that best described her.

Timothy felt threatened by any signs of independence. Despite his tough exterior, beneath the surface, he was a frightened young man. He did not want to lose his family, and attempted to keep that from happening. He periodically used force, intimidation, and degradation. Having said that, Timothy was a hard worker, a terrific father; and coached soccer as well.

Desiree had managed to go back and get her high school diploma. She loved styling hair as a young girl, and knew that was what she wanted to do. She went to school to become a cosmetologist. She opened her own business in the mid eighties, and Timothy and Desiree decided to divorce. It was time for both of them to go their separate ways. Though she wanted her independence, there was separation anxiety for a period of time. It was like a death in her family, and she sometimes felt it would have been better if one of them had died. She was determined to break loose, and to be on her own. Desiree and Timothy maintained as close a friendship as two divorced people could.

She began dating, remembering Timothy's last warning; all guys are dogs.

Having never really dated before, she was bound to make a few mistakes along the way. After all, isn't that why we date? There was the "Fabio" type. Mike, he had long hair, blue eyes and a smooth line. Next was Dan, who did not have a serious bone in his body. Their relationship had produced her third son, Jake. Jason was sixteen and Jett was fourteen at the time. She loved Jake dearly, but they struggled to make ends meet. Being a mother came naturally to her, while relationships seemed foreign. Her father had passed away when she was a young girl. Desiree did not have a role model to draw from. She would learn from trial and error.

This book is about setting boundaries. It is about discovering personal weaknesses, forgiveness and healing.

Desiree's boundaries were too loose and she had a tendency to allow people to get too close, leaving herself wide open to predators. However, Desiree discovered, when boundaries are too tight, no one gets in. In a healthy situation, there is balance. With balance, we can live a fulfilling life.

There were members of her family who had one or the other. Desiree Peters fell into the category of having boundaries that were too loose and maybe, at some points, having none at all.

Drugs and/or alcohol destroyed some of them; some became food addicted and ill; some became relationship addicted, which left them open to physical, emotional, and mental abuse.

Any, or all, of these addictions had the same outcome, and that was the destruction of what they could have become and contributed to the world. Desiree found that it is never too late.

Most members of her family had a high IQ, or intellectual quotient, giving all of them the opportunity to lead successful lives. However, their EQ, or emotional quotient, was low, creating drama and chaos, preventing them from success and happiness. A balance of both boundaries and emotional quotient was required to have stability in their lives. She told her children as they were growing up, not too much or too little; always strive to stay in the middle.

This is where Desiree believed good parenting is necessary. In her case, her parents did the best they could with what they knew. Ultimately as adults, everyone was accountable for their own choices.

This writing is a story within a story. It is a fictional story about Desiree Peter's life, beginning with her grandparents, and the correlation between their lives and hers. This is a love story, a mystery and a self-help book.

In the beginning of a dangerous relationship, if you feel something is wrong – it is. He/she may begin to say opposite things to confuse you. They may say you did not see what you saw, did not hear what you heard, and do not know what you know. They intertwine this behavior with wonderful acts of generosity kindness and romance to keep you guessing. You will question yourself, and begin to believe you might be crazy. They attempt to make you dependent on them. This is a gradual process which you cannot see coming. They slowly murder your ability to make rational decisions and then take your soul.

Desiree had many red flags and relationships to show her she needed to tighten her boundaries; all of which she ignored, and with every situation, her experience grew worse. She guessed it was true that you cannot see the picture once you are inside the frame, and that which does not kill you will make you strong. The answer is to learn early so we do not waste precious time.

Early in a dangerous relationship, seventy-five percent of what he/she tells you will be true, while the rest will be lies. Every time they get away with it, the percentage begins to change. Eventually seventy-five percent will be lies, while only twenty-five percent will be true. They intertwine truth with lies, leaving you to believe; well he/she told the truth about this so that must be true – maybe I am crazy! Some see right through them, so they just keep moving on until they find another victim.

They have games going on in isolated areas; keeping their options open. If you feel you are being isolated from certain people, towns, or places there is a reason for that; he/she does not want these two worlds to collide. In the end, Desiree was given the simplest advice and only answer – in order to heal and move on. Even though, in the beginning, she did not really want out, no matter what she said, she would eventually face the edge of insanity.

The answer came from her sister Brianna long before Desiree took her advice, "Desiree, if you had money he would have already married you. He is arrogant and has always thought he was better than you are. You are as good looking a woman as he is a man, and a much better person than he will ever be. I would not spit on the best part of him. Just think of him as dead, and please never speak to him again."

No contact is the one and only answer. He/she may try to keep contact to confuse you and maintain control.

Please have blind faith that this is true and keep the faith. They are very charming, tenacious, romantic, creative, and clever in the ways they maintain control. Whatever it takes – do it!

At first, it will be like looking through binoculars with the lens cover on. Then, when it comes off, the vision will go from blurry to clear – that I promise!

Not only have you been hurting those around you; you suffer as well. If you do not stop, there will be no one around when it is over. That includes friends, co-workers, and even family. Do not seek revenge and I know how tempting and strong this desire is. Walk away while you have time left to be happy and repair the damage so you can find the life you were supposed to have. Take it back. In the end, he/she will live a sad and lonely life, and when you no longer care about how his/her life turns out, you will know you are on your way out.

During this period of healing, do not make any major decisions that could put you in debt or make the healing process more difficult, because then he/she wins again.

If you cannot walk away or confront them, please keep a journal, not only of strange things but also of everything that happens. Wait a few weeks to read it, and keep doing this until you prove to yourself what is really happening.

When relationships begin, two worlds collide and when they do – we learn. Sometimes I find we learn from each other and grow, or we learn from each other and leave. Either way, we are becoming the whole person we were meant to be.

She could not undo her past but she could change her future, and while her future was much shorter than it was when her story began, she began looking forward, and her goal was to be in the here and now as much as possible. She was learning to be with herself. Her future was always in her hands and not someone else's.

I dedicate this book to Jereme, Josh, and Jared; I love you as big as the sky. I hope you know how much – I think you do. While I feel I have done well as your mother, I am also human, having made many mistakes in my personal life. I love each of you the same and I admire each of you for different reasons. You are truly the loves of my life. All three of you make me proud to be your mom. You are living your lives impeccably and when I leave this world, I know I have contributed in a positive way to the world through each one of you. Please pay it forward.

Mom

To my family, friends, and my clients, I love you and thank you for your support, professionally and personally, for allowing me to dump on you time after time. I thank you for all of your advice and encouragement even though I did not listen most times; it has been a tremendous help to me in my attempts to heal.

I have been going to Siesta Key, the place I love, for the past couple of years to relax and write and write and write. My budget has not always allowed for these trips, but going there has been priceless in terms of healing. I have finished this story, and I hope to help someone out there who is going through a similar circumstance. It is just after sunset and a beautiful one at that, and I am taking my last walk along the beach, allowing the warm tide to roll over my feet and savoring the beauty of this place.

I can now see the beauty in simple things. This has been the first time I can recall leaving home and I am not worrying about anything or anyone. I am taking each day as it comes. My head, my heart, my body, and soul feel so light I could fly!

In an attempt to discover where Desiree was going, she felt she needed to look back at where she came from, how she got there and whom she was; therefore, she started at the beginning.

There had been wonderful moments in her life, even the relationships she so poorly chose had moments of pure bliss. She learned something from every experience; she wished she could have learned sooner.

Desiree had a strong personality; some might say stubborn. She had always been curious; some might say nosy. While these characteristics helped her through this journey, those same characteristics also put her on that road.

It reminded her of her favorite movie, 'The Wizard of Oz'. Dorothy was curious about other places and surely, she thought, there was something and somewhere better than where she was. She, along with Toto, set out on that journey down the yellow brick road to find a better place, only to find herself having to make a choice. 'Which path should I take?' she wondered, while the wise Scarecrow, who did not possess a brain, told her she would have to decide for herself. She made her choice, and before she knew it, she was running into witches, monkeys, and evil apple trees. In the end, she made it back home, and promised when she set about trying to find her heart's desire she would look no further than her own back yard.

She also realized she had the power within her to make her own choices and create her own destiny. She got where she wanted to go although there may have been an easier path. She made her choices and hoped she had learned from her mistakes. Then there was Desiree.

Something her mother innocently told her was deeply seared in her brain "Desiree Peters, you will always learn everything the hard way."

Just as teaching your child manners, etiquette, and so on, you teach them by your words, and the way you live your life. If children are to believe you when you say "Mind your manners, Do your homework, You need to rest" then why would they not believe everything else you tell them?

Negative words such as;

"Fat, ugly, clutsy, stupid, bad. You will never amount to anything," (and the list goes on) will become a part of who your child believes they are, and they may waste a lifetime learning it is not true.

When I began writing this book, my name was Deborah Rainwater. On the day I completed this story, as I was walking on the beach, I made my decision. I would change my name back to the one given at birth and start over. My name is Deborah Porter

If after reading this, you believe this could never happen to you, guess again. I suggest you read books by M. Scott Peck, M.D. and Robert D. Hare, PhD

This book is based on a true story. Any similarities to any persons living or dead are purely coincidental.

I wrote this when Jereme and Josh were small, around 1980.

Life As I Know It

Time passes by slowly
Life is gone quickly
New water is pure
Old rivers become polluted

New, soon becomes old
Time makes old become new
Spring brings fresh green color
Soon to become brown

Children become adults
Adults never grow old

Soft lineless skin
Becomes filled with roughness and age
Long silky hair
Soon becomes brittle and gray

Rarely traveled country roads
Soon become familiar pathways
With many years of age
Youth is far behind
But never forgotten

Do not look back, only forward
For life is like fine wine

Deborah M. Rainwater

Friday February 13th, 1992

I reached out my hand
And led the way
I watched you grow
More independent every day
I turned around
You are almost grown
And in no time at all
You will be on your own
I have done the very best that I can
To make sure you will become
A very special man

I have made many mistakes
Along the way
But you have assured me
Everything will be okay

I have a new son
And you have a new brother too
How lucky he is
To have brothers like you

I never knew men could be so small
But with all we've been through
In my eyes, you are tall

When all is said and done
I have given life
To three beautiful sons

"I Love You As Big As the Sky"

Mom
Deborah M. Rainwater

Jared

I love you
With all of my heart, you see
Since Jereme and Josh are grown
It's been only you and me

You are handsome
Thoughtful and incredibly smart
You have always been
From the very start

You are brave
And you are kind
Although as your mom
I intuitively know
What is on your mind

You would make
Any one proud
To call you son
And to me
You will always be
Number one

Remember
Some of the greatest lessons learned
Are what not
To ever do
To any of those
Who love you
And have earned

The right to be loved by you
In return

I have made some poor choices
Along the way
You were not one of them
I thank God
That I have you
Every day

Mom

Chapter 1

She made up her mind that she would date anyone who asked, but she was finished with relationships. Previous relationships had always disappointed her. She was certain her knight in shining armor was just around the corner.

Jonathon Peters, known as John was born to a poor family in the late nineteenth century, where he grew up in the hills of Kentucky. He met and married Myrtle Bell, born in the early twentieth century. Her family was also poor. She grew to become a beautiful woman but suffered from depression. Together they had four children, John born 1920, Noreen born 1922, Becker in 1924, and Joy in 1926. Jonathon was a hard worker who worked day in and day out in the fields, to try to keep a roof over their heads. There was not much work in the hills of Kentucky, so they headed north to Wisconsin, settling on a farm in White Lake.

James William O'Donnell was born in Ireland around 1871. He grew up in Nova Scotia, then in Muskegon, Michigan, before finally settling in Tomahawk, Wisconsin. James suffered from polio as a young boy that left him with a noticeable limp. He married a woman named Marie. Sadly, she passed away in 1914. It was unknown why Marie passed at such an early age. In those days the reasons for a death at an early age, was merely a guess. He remarried late in life after meeting a woman, whom it was rumored was a mail order bride, named Ella Hamilton.

Ella was a rather plain looking woman and had two grown children from a previous marriage to John Jollands. Her family was originally from Scotland, but Ella was born in Battle Creek, Michigan, and raised in Grand Rapids, Michigan. She and John had two children, Roy and Helen. That marriage ended when John passed away in 1921. She traveled to Wisconsin and settled with James in the town of Elcho, near Tomahawk. They had two children together, Dorothy Marie in 1922, and Grace Ella in 1926.

James, who came from a long line of saloonkeepers, was not much of a worker due to his limitations from the polio. However, he was quite a good drinker. He was a sawmill worker and became the Justice of the Peace in that small town; a fact that made Grace quite proud, but then again so did everything he did.

As John was from the South, and Grace from the North, they had no idea their worlds would collide. Ella became bedridden when Grace was very young. The family suspected that she may have suffered from colon cancer, and history would repeat itself. The only memories Grace had of her mother, were her being in bed and very sick. She passed away in early spring of 1938 from Pulmonary Thrombosis, just before Grace turned 12. Her sister, Dorothy was 16.

Having your loved one at home after they passed was common back then. Grace had vivid memories of being at her house; backed in a corner, as a frightened observer, as people flowed in and out to view her mother. She did not understand what was happening and no one bothered to explain.

Dorothy was an Irish red head, with a wild streak and a temper to match, while Grace was a raven-haired beauty with a docile demeanor. James spent most of his time in taverns; Grace and Dorothy raised themselves. Dorothy took that as an opportunity to run wild while Grace spent a lot of her time trying to keep track of her father. Usually she would find him at the local tavern, begging him to come home, if she could only fix him. John on the other hand was a somber, curious boy and somewhat mischievous at the same time. His family lived on a farm and they passed the time away playing cards. John also spent a lot of time playing pranks on his younger siblings. He kept a distance from people. He purposely intimidated everyone he met and continued to do so his entire life.

Myrtle sent the boys to CC camp, an organization that paid young men to do community service, make a little money and to keep out of trouble. Dorothy met Becker while he was working in the area and took a liking to him. That romance was short lived and she settled for his older brother, John.

They married and had a baby shortly after who, unfortunately, died. Her parents named her after her aunt Grace. They had three more children, Diana Louise in March of 1941, John Jr. in April 1942, and Will Coleman in November 1944. During that time, Grace's father told her he could no longer take care of her. The state had taken their house and she would have to find work and live on her own. She and a childhood friend, Florence ventured to Michigan to find work. They received food and shelter in exchange for being dishwashers at a hotel.

She eventually went to visit Dorothy and John; however, this is where her memory becomes fuzzy. Dorothy divorced John, leaving him with their three children. John sent them to stay with relatives, while he worked. He went to Indiana to look for better work, while Diana and John Jr. suffered abuse at the hands of the relatives. A family named Chandling adopted Will the youngest, with the understanding his father could visit.

While living with Jonathon and Annie, their paternal grandfather and step grandmother, John and Diana's food was severely rationed, John's chore was to feed the dogs the remaining food after dinner, and would happily do so. He ate with them. He also began stealing other boy's lunches at school, which landed him in trouble.

By this time, Grace was involved with John and was pregnant. She would send gifts to Diana and John but they would disappear.

Grace gave birth to her first child, a girl, Brianna Joyce in January of 1947. She was their pride and joy. Brianna was exotic looking and a beautiful girl, with dark skin, thick dark hair, and large, haunting eyes.

Shortly thereafter, John left Grace to marry a young girl named Jenny. He had asked Grace to leave, but she refused. He told her to wait for him, as he would be back. John and Jenny married and moved across the street. True to his word after a year, he divorced Jenny and came back. In the meantime, Grace was working at a good paying job and was doing fine without him. She let him come back; one of the many bad choices she made and there were many more to follow.

They finally sent for Diana and John. Grace tried to help take care of them as they had worn out their welcome at their grandfather's and needed to be with their parents.

Up to that point, Brianna had been the princess, while Diana, although a pleasant looking girl was plump with fine hair and no match for Brianna. From the beginning, she was jealous and understandably so. She would do anything to get her father's attention. It did not matter if the attention was positive or negative as long as she got it. Around 1950 the family packed up and moved to a small town, just outside of Gary, Indiana.

It was a small house with an outside toilet. There were two bedrooms, one for John and Grace; leaving one for the four children to share.

Grace was in her early twenties, trying to take care of her own daughter and two of John and Dorothy's children. She was also working and trying to keep track of John's whereabouts, which was no easy task. She was under tremendous stress but tried to control it. To add to this she became pregnant again and in October 1952 gave birth to Katy Lynn. Grace left her job; she had her hands full and had more than enough to do at home.

While Grace got along well with John Jr., Diana was another matter. Diana seemed to hate Brianna and was jealous of the bond she and John shared. This made her more than determined to do anything to get attention. On July 7, 1955, John decided to do the

4

right thing; he married Grace. After all, they had two children, another two of his, and she was now pregnant again. Seven months later, in February of 1956, she gave birth to yet another girl, Desiree Marie. This is where her story begins.

Chapter 2

John, along with his regular job as a hammer smith at a forging plant, decided to open a pool hall. It was a front for the poker games he organized in the backroom. He was a very private but imposing man and, kept his distance from people by intimidating them. He enjoyed the power it gave him. He was stuck with an ever-growing family, as was Grace.

They had moved again by the time Desiree was eighteen months old. The house was only two streets from where they were living before. It was bigger, had three bedrooms, and yes it did have an inside bathroom. There were children everywhere and no place to go to get away from the chaos.

John could go to work, the pool hall, or the bars to get away, but Grace had no place to go. She had no space of her own and no activities she could look forward to outside of the home. Grace had long since reached her boiling point and was bubbling over more and more. She felt trapped by the life they had created.

She believed there was no way out, and was emotionally and physically abused. It was the late 1950s and a different time back then; and yes – she was pregnant again. In May 1958, she had her first son, Reagan Matthew. When the time came, John dropped her off at the hospital and told her to call him to let him know if it was a boy or girl.

In November 1960, Grace had yet another boy, Braden David. Brianna was there to help with the younger ones and did the best she could. Less than two years later, in March, 1962, she gave birth to her last child, Raquel Jean.

By then they had moved again to the other side of town a few miles away. They were living in a much larger house on 45th Street. It was huge, old and run down but to them it was the best. They were able to have their own rooms; well at least they only had one roommate. The children had a big yard to play in and John even planted a garden.

Although they had more space, Grace had long since reached her limit, and had taken to raging outbursts that would send the children scattering like roaches when the lights come on. John always seemed unaffected and as calm as the cucumbers in his garden. He was rarely at home, sometimes leaving for days at a time.

Desiree remembered when she was about ten; John had done one of his disappearing acts when the tail end of a tornado was passing through. The storm was so violent the huge trees in their yard were bending with the wind and rain. None of them was able to sleep and the electricity was out. Like cars on a train, they were linked together, each holding onto the one in front. They carried a flashlight, going from room to room, looking out of the windows. Not only were they waiting for the storm to subside, they desperately wanted their dad to come home. That was her first memory of feeling let down and unsafe. Many times in the middle of the night, Desiree would drift back off to sleep after hearing her father's cough. It was music to her ears.

Grace was an emotional prisoner and very angry about the trap she was in. She would slowly boil in reaction to John's behavior and her rage would suddenly explode like a volcano from the pent-up pressure. She seemed to target certain ones. She would throw things through the walls, using her fists, shoes, whatever was within reach. The main targets were Brianna, Desiree, and Reagan. While no one was safe, she would, or so it seemed seek them out, either that or the others were smarter and faster than they were.

They would hear the opening and closing of cabinet doors and then it would turn into slamming (Desiree likened it to drumming). There was the clanging of the metal grills on the stove that turned into banging with every slam of her fist.

At the time, it was not funny. John had long since realized Grace was trapped and was very confident she would never leave him – no matter what he did. There was not much he did not test her with.

Grace spent her days scrubbing floors, doing laundry, and preparing their next meal. Desiree was always amazed at how her mother could peel an apple or a potato in one continuous corkscrew; Grace would always give her a slice to hold her over until dinnertime. There was little, if any time, to teach the children manners, etiquette, or anything else that most take for granted. They were left to teach themselves and to help the younger ones. Since they had no idea what they were doing, they did not do a very good job.

Grace was as loving as she was mean, which always confused Desiree. There were times when she would literally pick her up by her hair and throw her onto the bed. Her confusion came when, late at night while she was still snubbing from crying hours earlier, she would sit on the edge of Desiree's bed, wiping the tears and brushing the hair from her forehead, saying, "Honey please don't cry, you will have bad dreams." Desiree could see the regret in her face and then Grace would say, "I love you more than all of the tea in China." She knew she loved her, at least for now. She remembered being knocked backwards into the bathtub but does not remember her mother showing any remorse that time.

Each of the children had their own story to tell and their own perceptions of the way things happened and certainly they vary somewhat, but all agreed that this was no way for anyone to have been treated. It did not give them many positive memories but there were some – just a few.

Desiree would sit for endless hours on a blanket she had spread beneath the big oak tree in Katy Groover's yard next door, dressing Barbie for her date with Ken. Katy did not allow Desiree to leave her yard with Barbie, and she would dream of having one of her very own.

In 1964, by the time Raquel was two years old, John Jr. had already married a girl named Brenna. Brianna and Dave lived a short distance away, so did John Jr. and Brenna, his wife at the time. Diana was on her second marriage and never lived long in one place. For unknown reasons she had a hysterectomy when she was nineteen but always wanted children. She would marry and divorce five times. After her failed relationship with John and her failed marriages, she continued to make many bad choices in her life. She suffered one illness and surgery after another.

John Jr. and Brenna had their first child, Devon Mark in July 1964, and Brianna and Dave, had Deon in May 1965. Will visited throughout the years and joined the service, landing him in the Vietnam War.

Every Sunday felt like a holiday to them. Grace prepared a big meal with all of the trimmings. She and Desiree would always bake a yellow cake from scratch and use their homemade old-fashioned fudge recipe as frosting. By the end of the day, half of the cake was gone and all of the fudge had been broken off the rest; they never did find out which bandit snuck in and stole it.

They made triangular hats from the newspaper John left behind, and then used them as weapons; beating each other with them. There were food fights and the younger ones sat in utter amazement, as the older ones settled in to play a game called Spoon. They made a little spending money serving them coffee or whatever else they wanted as they were always too involved to leave the table.

It was a good day if nothing was broken, that is, until John came home. Then the party was over. Everyone packed up their belongings, their kids and went home. Desiree lived for Sundays.

Those were great times and having some of the kids out of the house lightened Grace's load. Her outbursts were less but at times, they still came vigorously.

Chapter 3

There were strange women at their house from time to time. One in particular stood out for Desiree. Her name was Bonnie; a wino John had found somewhere. She did not have a place to stay and much to Grace's chagrin; he brought her home. As time passed there was a new addition, her son Mark. He appeared, or so it seemed, out of nowhere. Bonnie was a lounge singer. Being the nosy one, Desiree had wandered upstairs to one of the bedrooms that had now become a storage area when Brianna had left home. She picked up a brochure lying on top of a box, and although she was barely recognizable, Desiree knew it was Bonnie. She had been beautiful. She was wearing a slinky dress and somewhat lying on a Baby Grand piano.

She spent hours on end with Katy and Desiree, trying to teach them to harmonize, and from what Desiree was later told, she did not do a very good job. She taught the girls to crochet rugs and to make a toy, which amounted to no more than a button on a string. Nevertheless, they would spend the entire day on these projects.

Grace tired of finding empty wine bottles in the laundry and other bizarre places, so demanded she leave. After hours of listening to her and Mark crying out on the lawn, and embarrassed the neighbors could hear, she relented and let them come back. The last memory Desiree had of Bonnie and Mark is watching them fade away as they walked down 45th Street, carrying everything they owned in a brown paper sack.

Then there was Ellen, whom it was rumored that John was the father of at least one of her children. There were times when they would come home, only to find her and John picking vegetables in their garden.

It was another wonderful day in the Peters household when John came home with the groceries. He always did the chores that took him away from home while Grace did everything in the house. As Grace removed the groceries she found hairspray among other items John would never purchase, Desiree did not stick around to see the outcome; everyone scattered. They paid for John's indiscretions because when she was angry the punishment came to them (chain of command, Desiree guessed).

This was Desiree's family and as crazy as the dysfunction was, it was all she knew. She was a busy body and very outspoken at times but Desiree loved all of them. She was fierce in her beliefs and had no problem standing up for what she felt was right, but she was as honest and loyal as one could be.

Ellen's kids would spend nights with them and later when John passed, Grace would take them to her house for visits. Was that forgiveness or ignorance; Desiree was not sure? Early on, John was also known to see Aunt Dorothy when she came to town. By then she was married to Uncle Delmar, a great person, with a wonderful sense of humor. After leaving John with his three children many years earlier, she had given birth to another boy. While the rumor was he was also John's, she put him up for adoption. She and Uncle Delmar had one son together, Rick. He was the only child she raised and the only one she ever claimed.

Grace seemed to roll with whatever John did, and nothing ever became bad enough to make her leave. She could not bear to have her family split up. She was always reminded of the state taking her childhood home, and being told by her father she would have to leave at the tender age of fifteen.

She loved her children and thought she was doing the right thing; she had been abandoned and was not about to let that happen to them. As warped as that seems, that was her perspective. Even still, she had forgiven her own father; he died at the age of 86, the year Desiree was born. Later, not long before she passed and as her health deteriorated, her anger toward John, surfaced. He had refused to take her to visit Granddad in the sanitarium, in Wisconsin. She confided in Desiree that her father despised their dad for ruining both of his daughter's lives. Her love and admiration for the man who abandoned her would follow her to the end of her days.

Chapter 4

It was early on Monday morning, May 8, 1967 when everything changed. There was a blood-curdling scream coming from the kitchen. Desiree remembered peering through the door that led from the living room to the kitchen. She saw her Dad's head resting on the table, appearing as though he had decided to take a nap. Then the neighbors were there, a stretcher and men carrying him out, and he was gone from her life.

Reagan turned 9 years old the following day, but there would not be a celebration. Desiree believed the sadness of losing his father never left him. Desiree did not remember feeling much of anything and at the time, never coming back meant nothing to her. John was 47; she was 11.

Grace still had stress-filled days but they were of a different kind. Sometimes it spilled over. She was left with five children, no money, and a rented house where they were eventually evicted. The property owner was not paying the mortgage and it was in foreclosure. She was babysitting for the neighbor's girls, while also receiving social security.

Grace went out and found a halfway decent job on an assembly line at a factory. They made camera parts, tripods, and so on. She would come home so excited when she made rate. Rate was a number given that required you to make at least that amount per hour. Anything over that, and you got a bonus and this added to your hourly rate. She would proudly display her bonus slips to anyone who would look.

Work became both her stress reliever and her social outlet. Although she was not perfect, she was happy and seemed to be a different person. Grace worked tirelessly to make ends meet. She kept a roof over the family's heads and food on the table; she had little time to teach them about life, and the other necessities that were foreign to her. You cannot expect to learn algebra when you do not know basic math. Her days were spent working; her nights were spent doing the laundry, cooking dinner, and paying bills. They were taking care of the younger ones, and they failed miserably.

Katy married Steven in December 1969, after quitting school at 16. They eventually settled in Tennessee; raising their family in the mountains. Desiree was now the oldest at home and thought she could help her Mom with some of the chores. Desiree would try to cook and clean while monitoring her brother's whereabouts. It did not take long for her to realize, while she felt she could fix everything that was broken, this job was more than a 13 year old could handle.

Grace did not welcome her services. Desiree made her job much more difficult by telling on Reagan and Braden for their indiscretions. Her theory was, "Desiree – you do not need to know everything, you need to leave well enough alone." She did not have time to police the boys, nor the patience to see that they were where they should be. She would say, "What you do not know will not hurt you." That is the way she lived; leaving the younger ones to wreak havoc in everyone's lives, especially their own.

In June 1971 at the age of 15, and after leaving high school after her first year, Desiree married Timothy, who by all accounts, was a juvenile delinquent. He was the typical bad boy all of the girls wanted; how lucky Desiree was to get him!

They went to Hannibal, Missouri and back in one day, taking Grace with them to sign for Desiree, as she was too young to get married in the state of Indiana. Looking back Desiree had no idea what she was thinking. Timothy had been pressuring her and she guessed Grace felt she would have one less child to worry about.

Desiree was the one who never played by her rules. She wanted to know everything that was going on, while Grace wanted to put her blinders on and know nothing. The first night Desiree remembers going home to the wonderful, little, mobile home they had rented to find she was homesick and wanted to see her mom. Many years later Raquel told Desiree their mother wailed like a wounded animal that night.

Desiree quickly became used to her independence and it never entered her mind that she was leaving her baby brothers and sister; she just wanted out.

Reagan was special to Desiree. She did not know what connected you to one person as opposed to another, but they were close. She always felt protective of him and he always felt she protected too much. He was a wonderful person but he had a dark side. He was charismatic, agile, funny, and very handsome. As a child he thought he was Evil Knievel one minute, and Richard Pryor the next. He made Desiree laugh and he made her cry.

The choices he made changed the course of Desiree's life forever. Reagan was always up to something he should not have been and she was always one-step behind him, trying to keep him straight. He never did anything harmful to anyone – only to himself. He would ditch school, smoke pot, get drunk, sneak out of the house to see girls; you name it, he tried it.

Reagan, as the rest of them, was very intelligent. His IQ was high, but emotionally he was unstable and that would prove to be lethal. He made it through his junior year, quit school and after many attempts to find work; Grace decided he should go into the service, one less kid to worry about. He did not fare well, was involved with drugs and, at some point, was stabbed repeatedly in the back at a party that had got out of control. He was hospitalized in Washington at the time. He never revealed the specifics of what happened. Desiree was saddened when she later thought about how he must have felt when no one went to see him.

One evening he called from another hospital and said someone had laced his beer with animal tranquilizers – PCP. They had found traces in his mustache. He later laughed and said he had lied and had knowingly taken it.

One drunken weekend he came home on leave and announced, just before he went back, he had married Suzanne, a girl in the neighborhood. They never lived together and she ultimately divorced him. "She had hard lips anyway," he later complained. Not so surprisingly, the Army honorably discharged him. He came back home.

He then met and later married, Deirdra, one of his best friend's ex-girlfriends. They moved to Biloxi, Mississippi. He worked on a rig with their nephew, Devon who already lived there.

Reagan had two children and loved them dearly. For the most part, his life was ordinary and he put his past behind him. He tried to be a loving husband and father but his demons followed him, and as all couples do, they struggled from time to time. They moved back to Indiana in 1983 to be closer to friends and relatives.

He took a job at the University of Illinois. Their oldest sister, Diana was an administrator for a well-known doctor there and she got him the job. At first, he was just a gopher, but before long, his curiosity got the better of him. He ventured down to the morgue where he became quite intrigued by the whole process. He observed autopsies and after assisting, became an autopsy supervisor. He would later receive letters of recommendation listing him as a pathologist by his colleagues, and the other doctors. He did not have a high school diploma but later received his G.E.D.

When his marriage began to crumble, so did he. He began to use drugs again and his life went downhill from there. When his wife found a bag of used hypodermic needles, their marriage was finally over. Reagan never did anything half way; he went straight to crack.

His health deteriorated and they diagnosed him with Hepatitis C. At the time, little was known about this particular strain and he chose to ignore his health, living as though it did not exist. Desiree guessed he felt as their mother did – ignore it and it will go away.

Braden was the next youngest after Reagan and his life was just as turbulent. He was very talented in sports, especially baseball. He had a great arm and some thought that with the proper guidance he was talented enough to pursue a possible career in this field.

He also quit high school and began working at the University of Illinois before Reagan did. He worked in the shipping department and did his job well.

He had been married and had two daughters. His drug of choice was alcohol. He too was divorced and lived back at home with Grace. His ex-wife dropped the girls off at Grace's one day and she never returned. Although Braden was living there, Grace took most of the responsibility for the girls, seeing that they had clothes, food, lunch money, and so on.

Braden began to drink at work and take advantage of Grace in every way; borrowing money that he never gave back and drinking more and more. Money and other things went missing all the time but she always made excuses for him. The family was sure he loved her but his personality changed dramatically when he was drinking.

Desiree's baby sister, Raquel was quiet and withdrawn from the start and she had to admit she did not remember much about her. She was 15 when she married Randy. They had three children together and divorced.

There was a bitter custody battle that resulted in Randy raising their sons. She married three times after that and had a daughter, Brea in her second marriage. Raquel was the last of nine children and probably did not get the attention she so badly needed.

Chapter 5

Timothy and Desiree had a marriage that was doomed from the start. They were children, both insecure with no direction. He was doing what boys do at 18 and did not have a clue about commitment.

He was a hard worker, but young and not ready to settle down. In 1973, they bought their first house; it was on Walnut Street, just a few houses from her Mom's house. Desiree was 17; he was 20. By most people's observation, Desiree was a pretty girl but Timothy seemed to need attention from other girls. She had a childhood friend, Tamara who, at that time, had a crush on Reagan. They still hung around together even though Desiree was married; in fact, they bought the house where she grew up.

She and some of her friends would come over from time to time and hang out. She had one friend named Chrissy, who was six feet tall, dark haired and overweight. Desiree never viewed her as a threat. She at least had enough confidence to know she did not have a chance with her husband.

Timothy and Desiree were talking one day and he mentioned that he felt sorry for her and thought they should take her in, as her mother had kicked her out of the house and she had no place to go. She thought nothing of it and Desiree agreed.

Chrissy was still in school and they provided her with lunch money and took care of her. She would occasionally mention how she felt that Timothy was like an older brother to her, and even though something felt odd about this comment, she pushed it back and went on.

There were times when Desiree would go to bed and they would stay up watching television. At first, she thought no more about it, but one night in particular, something did not feel right, and she got back out of bed to find that Chrissy was on the couch. Timothy was sitting by her on the floor, and with uneasy feelings she went back to bed; after all what could she accuse them of doing. Finally, she moved back home and Desiree was happy about her decision.

The following Saturday evening Desiree jumped in the Blazer and went to the local K-Mart to buy some paint as they were painting one of the bedrooms. Chrissy was at their house and asked if she would drop her off at the corner near her house on the next block. She did and for some reason turned around and went right back home.

When Desiree walked in the back door, she heard Timothy say, "Someone's here, I have to go." He was hanging up the phone when she came in the living room. She asked whom he was talking to and he said Chrissy had called. They argued about that, and he told her she was too jealous, and gave a lame excuse as to why she had called. She let it go.

Timothy was working the day shift at the steel company. Desiree was home cleaning when the phone rang. It was Tamara's older sister, who she knew, but with whom she rarely spoke. They were having a casual conversation when suddenly she began talking about a friend of hers. Her husband was cheating on her, and she asked for Desiree's advice. She said, "The problem is he's cheating with another friend of mine."

Desiree told her she would tell the friend being cheated on. She proceeded to do just that. She said Desiree was that friend and thought she should know. She told her that it had started when he would leave for work. He would then call off and take a group of people to the beach. Chrissy was one of them.

Desiree was furious; so angry she scared herself. She called Timothy at work and demanded he come home immediately, if not sooner. He did. This was the first time she identified with the rage that boiled over in her mother.

Of course, he was sorry and it would never happen again. Like Mom, Desiree too felt trapped. At 17, she was married, without a job and did not even have a high school diploma. Where could she go and what could she do – so Desiree stayed.

They decided to make a fresh start. They sold their house and bought another, 50 miles away in the country. Timothy and Desiree got a dog, and for a time, they were happy, going fishing on his days off and enjoying their lives. While she was not over what had happened, they went on.

They met their new neighbors and would go over and play cards; everything was okay once again.

Desiree found out that she was pregnant and they were elated. She dreamed of becoming a mother. In February 1976, right after Reagan had joined the Army, she gave birth to a beautiful, little boy. They named him Jason Michael. Desiree was barely 20 years old, but she took to motherhood like a fish to water.

Less than a year later, she was pregnant again, and even though he was not planned, in November 1977; they welcomed Jett Matthew.

Desiree did not think she could love anyone the way she loved Jason, but she did. Three weeks after Jett was born, Timothy came to her and said he did not want to be married anymore and they separated.

She packed the babies and herself up, both of which were still in diapers, and he took them to her mom's house. Just before Christmas Eve, he reconsidered and came to take them home. Desiree knew that day their marriage was over, and somehow, someway she was going to leave him; but it would take over ten years.

She did not love him anymore. However, at the same time she made that decision, he decided he loved her and tried to be the husband she had always wanted – but it was too late.

Chapter 6

Over the years that followed, they had good times. They loved their boys. Desiree tried to get that feeling back but hard as she tried – it was gone. When Jett was about a year old, Desiree got a part-time job in an exclusive men's store and she loved it. She made friends and, for the first time, realized that there was a big world out there.

Her best friend there was an older, Italian woman, Margaret, who was as much fun as anyone her age. After work, once or twice a month, they would go to The Patio, a restaurant nearby to have Soganaki. They would listen to the band, sometimes late into the night. Desiree remembered there were times if Margaret got home too late her husband would lock the screen door so she would have to wake him up to get in. They would just laugh about it and do it again the next time.

While continuing her friendship with Margaret, Desiree decided to go to cosmetology school. She had always loved doing hair and decided that is what she wanted to do. She went back to her high school, got her GED, and then entered cosmetology school.

Jason and Jett were now approaching school age so Desiree thought this was a good time to go. She still wanted out but would have to educate herself and get a job in order to take care of her family.

Desiree met a girl in class that her family had known since she was small. Her name was Abby. She became a life-long friend. Abby was going through a divorce, and Timothy and Desiree had separated. They had sold their house in 1980, and the boys and Desiree had moved in to an apartment close to her cosmetology school. Timothy was living with his mother.

She concentrated on school and the boys and even though she had her share of fun, Timothy wasted no time living the nightlife.

They reconciled by the time she had finished school in 1981. Within a year, they had purchased a small house, and tried to start over. The boys were now in school and they were teaching them how to play soccer. Everything was going well.

Desiree wanted to open her own salon and tried to find a partner. She had met a sweet girl, Jackie at cosmetology school. She was a good stylist and she decided to join her venture. Desiree was excited.

The new salon opened in 1986 and business was good from the start. By the beginning of 1988, Desiree had built a little self-esteem and once again, Timothy and she had separated. Desiree finally filed for divorce. They continued to live near each other and still coached the boys together.

Despite everything, they had wonderful children, and they tried to keep them that way. Timothy was controlling and had a temper that would sometimes erupt in physical and verbal abuse, and constant manipulation. At the same time, Desiree was becoming more independent and stubborn, and at times, she fueled the fire.

As they had known each other since they were kids, letting go was not easy. While being newly single was exciting, it was also very scary. Desiree had to learn to date.

Timothy seemed to have less trouble dating; he dated and dated and dated. Every time Desiree would find out about someone he was dating; she would be hurt. By the time that hurt was subsiding, there would be another, and eventually it stopped.

Two years prior to their divorce, Desiree had received flowers anonymously at work and she remembered the card saying, "Just a little sunshine on a somewhat rainy day." While it felt good to get a little attention, she had no idea who had sent them.

While Desiree was out of town, Abby and Timothy had decided they would investigate. Timothy found out, through manipulating the florist that one of Desiree's clients had sent them. Mike had never mentioned this to her; he was married. However, during their divorce he came in to get his haircut. Desiree was surprised when a mutual acquaintance had informed her that Mike had a six-month-old son and had wondered why he never told her. She asked him if there was something he had forgotten to mention, and he said, "Yes, I'm going through a divorce." She was shocked once again. He asked Desiree if she would have lunch with him and finally she relented.

They began dating and she was infatuated. He wined and dined her, taking Desiree places she had never been.

Although Timothy had been dating, he was very upset to find out she was too. When he found out who it was, he was furious. He insisted on meeting him and Desiree arranged it. When he came back from the meeting, he simply said, "Just remember all guys are dogs."

Mike and Desiree had had walks to the Chicago River, horse and buggy rides in the city, and dinners at fine Italian restaurants. They went dancing, and while it was fun, it was short lived.

Eventually his wife called her salon to find out whom he was dating, because she had found the number on her phone bill. Then it was pretty much over for them.

Apparently, Mike would call Desiree long distance from her house while watching his son. Shortly after, he came to Desiree and said he was going back to his wife because he could not leave his son.

He was a fantasy with long hair, piercing blue eyes and a free spirit, and just like that – he was gone. She continued with her divorce and Mike would occasionally call but he no longer came to the salon. Eventually the calls stopped and Desiree moved on.

Her divorce was final in 1989. She was preparing to open her second salon in a nearby town – without a partner this time. Desiree had been in a partnership with Jackie, whose parents had financially backed her and were involved in every decision they made. Because she was going through a divorce and emotionally unstable at the time, Desiree decided, she did not want a partner in her new adventure.

As Desiree was the one that had done most of the work putting the first salon together, She felt she had the Midas touch and could easily do it again. Unfortunately, Desiree was wrong.

A legal battle ensued with her existing partner and as she was under so much stress because of her divorce and the new salon, she sold out to her partner. Looking back, it was another bad choice.

Chapter 7

Desiree moved forward with her business adventure and then began a new relationship.

Once a week, Desiree and her friends would go to a bar in another town, mostly for the entertainment. They had a lip sync contest every Thursday and the girls got a big kick out of watching people. While some were creative, others just made fools of themselves. Before she knew it, the girls had decided that they could do better and signed up.

They put on their black make-up, made their dresses, and before Desiree's eyes, they transformed into Aretha Franklin and her back-up singers. They took first place, became the favorites at the bar, and won $500.

On one of these Thursdays, a regular at the bar came over to their table. He told Desiree his friend wanted to meet her. She went by the bar on the way to the restroom to check him out and decided he was not her type.

He had black, curly hair and was a big man. Desiree was usually attracted to blonde haired, blue eyed, slender men. He came over and introduced himself, "Hi, my name is Dan, and you are?"

"Desiree, it is nice to meet you." He asked her to dance, and they did. Down the road, one of her clients would remind her. "See I told you, you should have danced all night."

While he was not her type, he was funny. Dan did not seem to have a serious bone in his body, very different from what she was used to. "I have a farm down the street and I'm having a hog roast this weekend if you'd like to come."

He took her number and the next day he called. Desiree thought, he is funny, attentive and maybe just what she needed right now. She did not want to be in a serious relationship.

Desiree pulled up to the farm that weekend around 9 pm and because she was driving a red Corvette, people came running over to see the new girl. "I'm looking for Dan; do you know where he is?"

"Yep, he's passed out on a lawn chair over there."

"Well, tell him Desiree stopped by."

"Do you want us to go get him?"

"No, just tell him I stopped by."

The next day he called and the next, flowers were delivered. He was fun and there was always a practical joke, and calls at 4 am while he was milking cows. He did not seem to have a care in the world.

He also wined and dined Desiree and, although she did not see him much due to the fact he worked twelve hours a day on the farm, he called often, and sent flowers and poetry on a regular basis.

In December of 1990, five months after they met, Dan asked if she would like to go to Florida with him to visit his sister. Desiree explained that while she would like to go, she could not leave her boys.

Shortly after, he informed her he had bought the tickets and she had to go. Dan and Desiree went and had a great time. There were Christmas lights on the palm trees swaying with the breeze. It was her first trip to Florida and Dan made everything fun. She met and liked his sister; Anita made her feel right at home.

She said she could not believe the difference in Dan since he had met her. Desiree was flattered, and Dan was beginning to grow on her. On his birthday in April 1991, he got the biggest birthday surprise he could ever imagine, but they did not find out until a few weeks later what it was.

He came over and spent the entire weekend, and they took advantage of the time they had together. On his birthday they conceived her third, and his first child, born in January 1992, Jacob Daniel. Dan was a confirmed bachelor and was never having children. He had been in a relationship with a girl named Tina. She had given him an ultimatum; he marries her, or she ends the relationship. It had ended.

Once again, Desiree's life was changing. While she had many more challenges to come, she also had a beautiful son.

Dan sent roses when they found out she was pregnant; red ones with tiny pink flowers sprinkled throughout. It was her guess he felt after two boys that Desiree wanted a girl, or maybe he did. She would be happy with another boy.

Almost at the end of her pregnancy, she called the farm and his dad answered, "Hello."

"This is Des, is Dan there?"

In a puzzled voice "Desiree, you aren't at the hospital?"

"No, I'm at home."

"Well, Dan got a call from a nurse who said you were there having the baby. He ran out of here and headed for the hospital."

Desiree laughed. One of his friends must have been paying him back for a practical joke he had played on them. Sure enough, his friends had convinced a bartender to call and say she was a nurse at Highland Community Hospital and that they needed him there a.s.a.p.

When it came time for Desiree to come home from the hospital, he picked her up in a van with his mother and her luggage. He put Jake and Desiree in the back seat, while his mother sat in the front with him. He dropped them off at Desiree's apartment (she had to give up her house, as she could no longer afford it with another baby coming and no maternity insurance) along with his mom. She was his substitute as he was unable to be there because he had cows to take care of.

His mother stayed only one day. Apparently, she wanted to take care of the baby while Desiree had assumed she was there to help with dinners and things so she could take care of him.

Four days after coming home the girls stopped by; it was a Thursday night. They had entered the lip sync contest once again. As she was unable to go, they performed for Jake and Desiree. They called when it was over to let her know they had taken second place. While they were taking turns talking to her, Desiree heard Dan yelling "Hi, Des," in the background. As she always said, he did not have a serious bone in his body.

Many things happened that year. When Jake was about five months old, she got a call about 7 am from one her girl's boyfriend, Gene. "Des, can you come to the salon, there's a problem?"

"What's going on?"

"Well, there's a fire in the store next door and they need your key."

"I'm in the shower but I will be right there."

"Can't wait that long. We're going to have to break the glass in the door so they can get in there," and that is exactly what they did.

Desiree rushed there only to find that they had everything under control but there was a lot of smoke damage. The roof was badly damaged and it was unsafe to open the salon. They had to remain closed until the roof was repaired.

Desiree called Dan, "The strip mall caught on fire this morning. I'm at the salon, can you come up and help with Jake so I can assess the damage, contact the girls and the insurance company and a half a dozen other things?"

"No I can't, I have chores to do."

"I can't believe you're not coming to help me. You're kidding, right?" He was not and he did not.

The repairs at the salon took a few months, and with absolutely no financial help from Dan, she kept on going. Things settled down and got back to normal.

On Jason's 17th birthday, Dan came over for cake and ice cream to celebrate. Afterwards they went out to play darts and while sitting there, Dan looked at her and said, "I guess I might as well just go ahead and marry you."

"That isn't funny, Dan."

"I mean it, I want to marry you."

Desiree was happy. Having a baby with someone and not being married was humiliating to her at the time, and getting married seemed to validate everything.

They went out that weekend. Desiree wanted to talk about their plans, and since Dan told her, they would go and pick the ring out on Monday, she asked about setting the date. "We'll get married in five years."

She could not believe what she had just heard and began laughing. They went to dinner and Desiree asked, "You are kidding, right?"

"No, I have to get a lot of things done and as far as my registered cows; they won't be ready to sell until then."

"No thanks." she replied.

That was the end of their relationship. He called a few months later and asked her if she would go with him to a dairy show in Wisconsin and she considered it. Grace called in her lunch hour, something she had never done before. "Honey, please don't go with him" so Desiree did not. It was over, but the battle was just beginning.

Chapter 8

The salon was open on Sundays, and one particular Sunday Desiree was working when a gorgeous man walked in, asking for a haircut. His name was Hank. He was tall with dark hair, blue eyes and a kind and beautiful smile, not to mention a body that belonged in Playgirl magazine. In no time, they had told each other about their lives and before she knew it; he was gone.

The next time he came in to have his haircut, one of the other girls cut it. As was always her policy to be friendly to their clients, they were talking back and forth when Desiree casually asked,

"What are you doing for the 4th?"

"I'm going to Chicago with my brother and his wife. How about you, what are your plans?"

Unaware of what her response implied, "I don't have any."

After his haircut he said, "Have a good day," and left.

The next evening one of the girls was coloring her hair and Hank stepped in the door. Desiree jumped up and ran to the back room. She looked terrible and did not want him to see her. He asked for Desiree and as she peeked around the corner, he asked,

"I was wondering if you would like to go with me for the 4th." The girls were nodding their heads and she said,

"Yes."

He came by the following night bringing pictures with him. He thoughtfully said,

"I want you to see the people we are going with." Wow, Desiree thought, what guy would do this?

30

Hank and Desiree's first date was a magical evening. They went to the city, spread a blanket along Lake Michigan, and while listening to music synchronized with beautiful fireworks; Desiree thought that just maybe, this was the right person for her.

Diana, Desiree's oldest sister, after many years of bad health and four open-heart surgeries had a massive heart attack and passed away in January of 1995. Desiree had lost her father at the age of eleven but up to that point, felt lucky to have such a large family with not many tragedies. Diana would come to Desiree's salon often to spend time with her and to look after Jake while she was working. Diana had many personal issues but was simply hilarious. She was the life of the party at many family gatherings. She would miss Diana.

Dan had gone back to Tina, the girl he had dated years before and had given him the ultimatum. She seemed hell bent on making Desiree's life miserable. The fact Desiree had a baby by Dan was more than she could bear.

They proceeded to level every accusation, including that Jake was malnourished and that she was abusing him. Anyone who knew Desiree knew that could not be further from the truth. She found that when another woman becomes involved with your ex, her insecurities, and the ex's desire for her to feel secure, could be volatile. Dan and Desiree went to court and she gained sole custody of her son. Afterwards, Tina had a baby with Dan and the fighting stopped; but Jake did not seem to fit in with their new family.

Desiree opened yet another salon near her apartment so she could be closer to home. It was not long before she decided to sell the bigger salon to one of her stylists and life became simpler. She was now nearer home and had fewer stylists. Desiree could also take Jake to work. Eventually as girls left, she was alone in the salon, but fortunately had a large enough clientele that she could manage.

Hank was perfect in every way but he bored Desiree to tears. He was physically beautiful and the only man she had ever been with that, no matter where they were, women would do a double take and then look to see who the lucky girl was.

He was gentle and very good to Jason and Jett but especially to Jake. He taught Desiree about appreciating the simple things around her. She had been too busy to see sunsets, trees, plants, and animals. Hank and Desiree would jog together and he noticed every little creature along the way. While she was thinking about the next thing she had to do, he was in the moment.

They would hike through the dunes or go to Chicago for a night out. Hank loved Jake and the feeling was mutual. They would fish in the pond by her apartment, play soccer, video games, or sit for hours with building blocks. There was no guesswork with him; he had an evenness that Desiree had never experienced in her life.

They were together for three and a half years. Nevertheless, it did not feel right to Desiree and, while he had asked her to marry him, they eventually ended the relationship the end of 1996. Desiree's difficulties felt normal to her and his evenness made Desiree feel something was missing.

She began to believe that her reason for being here was to be a mother, to teach her boys all of the things she had not been taught. Desiree was trying to supply them with all of the tools they would need to be loving, kind men who would someday contribute much more to the world than she would ever be capable of contributing.

Desiree was so proud of them and the job that she was doing as a mother, and at the same time, accepting she was a failure in relationships. Desiree was making all the wrong decisions and choosing the wrong men. The one she should have held on to, she let go. Hank and Desiree were in touch for a while and eventually she moved on and he married. He deserved happiness and Desiree hoped he found it.

Chapter 9

Desiree was in the salon and her tanning client, Dane, who she thought was an arrogant jerk, came in. They were talking, and he asked,

"Hey, would you like to go with me to watch one of my horses race tonight?" Sure, she thought. 'I have nothing better to do.' It was fun and a lot more excitement than she had had in a long time.

They continued to see each other and it was nice dinners with Dom Perione. Desiree could begin to like this. However, Dane had an ex-girlfriend who began to follow them, and would call Desiree from time to time. She continued even though red flags were flying everywhere. He did not have children and did not seem to like them either. She thought he would come around, and who could not like her boys. He tried but he never did, and while they were engaged for a short time, it ended.

Desiree made up her mind that she would date anyone who asked but she was finished with relationships. She did date around for a while: the blackjack dealer at a Las Vegas night who was telling her when to bet and fold. Mr. USA and a client who was just funny. She went out with friends, but in her heart, she still hoped she would be swept off her feet. She was finally feeling good about herself, working out and feeling genuinely content with her life. One day out of the blue, there he was the last thing Desiree expected, the love of her life.

It was the beginning of another summer, 1999. Jason had graduated college and married his high school sweetheart, Cassie in

October of 1998. Jett was going to I.U. at the time and was dating a girl he met there, Megan. She would eventually become a part of the family as well. Jake was an only child in terms of being the one left at home. Jason left when he was two and Jett when he was four.

Desiree's neighbor, Denise was a single mom with a son the same age as Jake. They had different lifestyles but a lot in common and became fast friends.

Denise was having new carpeting installed throughout her apartment and Desiree stopped by to lend a hand. They spent the evening getting things off the floor so it would be ready for the next day when the installers came.

The following morning she went to the gym as usual. She pulled into her parking space and when she got out of the car, there were two guys standing in front of Denise's place. Desiree thought these must be the guys she said would be coming to move the heavy things for her.

She glanced over and one of them was Dan, a friend of Denise's from work. They began teasing one another and she went on to her apartment. Desiree needed a shower and then she would go over and see if Denise needed her help.

She went over and they seemed to have everything under control but she could not help noticing that the other guy was rather good looking. Jokingly she whispered, "How do you find all of these good looking guys to help you?" and they laughed.

He did not seem to be paying any attention whatsoever to her. He appeared to be a million miles away. She decided she was not needed and went back home to do her cleaning and laundry. It was her day off and she had catching up to do. A short time later Denise called and asked,

"Hey do you want to go to Checkers with us for lunch? It's my treat since you helped me." Feeling a little overwhelmed, Desiree said,

"You go ahead. I have things to catch up on, but thanks for asking."

Later that day, Desiree stopped by to see if she wanted her to help put things back. That handsome, quiet man was there for the same reason. Oddly enough, Denise did not introduce them, and he left. Desiree could not help but notice,

"Nice butt"

"Denise replied, "You should go out with him. He is married, but in name only. His wife has a boyfriend and they're living in the same house, but leading separate lives."

In disbelief Desiree retorted,

"Are you kidding me? I am not going out with a guy who is married – end of story."

Denise came home the next evening from her bartending job and said,

"Guess who was asking about you today?" He was a regular there and usually met his father-in-law for lunch.

Desiree said,

"No way," and thought nothing more of it.

A few days went by and Denise called and suggested,

"Let's take Nicky and Jake to Benchwarmers for lunch. We will eat in the restaurant side and maybe they can play video games. I really need to do something with Nicky and I thought it might be fun if Jake came along."

"Sure we'll go. It sounds like a good idea."

So on Monday, their day off, they took the boys to Benchwarmers for lunch. They were all having a great time, the food was good, and the boys seemed to be enjoying it. An older man then came from the bar into the restaurant and stopped by their table to say, hello.

"Desiree this is Mr. Bevan, Mr. Bevan this is my friend Desiree."

"It's nice to meet you Desiree. Enjoy your lunch." Shortly after he left, in walks the handsome man who had helped Denise move her furniture, imagine that!

"I was on my way out and I wanted to say hi."

"Zach this is Desiree, Desiree this is Zach."

"Hi, and who do we have here?" he said as he looked Jake's way.

"This is Jake." As he offered to shake his hand,

"Nice to meet you, Jake, go on with your lunch. I have to go, have a good day."

Desiree realized this lunch date was a set up.

She went on with life as usual, finally getting over her past and feeling good about her future. One day, while at the salon, Zach stopped by to drop off some fresh vegetables. However, just like that, he was gone.

Before long, she was seeing him more and more. On Saturday, Denise asked if Desiree would meet her at Benchwarmers to listen to one of her favorite bands. Desiree explained she had invited her family and friends over for the following day.

About eight o'clock that night she jumped in the shower. What the heck – I am going. She wore her baby blue sleeveless top with her denim skirt. I may as well show off for as long as I can, she thought. I am 43 and who knows how much longer I have before this body falls apart.

Denise was in full swing when Desiree got there and she was somewhat relieved when she saw Zach at the bar. At least she could talk with someone. The bar was packed and the music was loud. He suggested they go into the other room so they could hear each other. He began telling Desiree a little about himself and she was thinking – boring. He likes to fish and hunt, whoopee! He did impress her however when he said his mother had been ill and he was taking care of her, that was a good sign. They did not stay out late as he explained he usually went to bed early. He walked Desiree to her car and simply said, "Goodnight" and he left.

She was happy to go home. She had a big day ahead and went straight to bed. By noon, her family was there but her girlfriends were not coming until the evening. They were visiting while grilling hotdogs and burgers when the phone rang.

"Hi Zach, how are you?"

"Fine, I invited some friends over today and they didn't show up. Do you mind if I drop this food off at your place? I don't want it to go to waste."

"Sure, if you want to and thanks, that's very nice of you."

He only lived a couple of blocks from Desiree, so a few minutes later he was at her door with grilled chicken and potatoes in hand. As she was guiding him through the living room out to the patio, she introduced him to family members who were getting ready to leave. By then, Desiree's girlfriends were there and when he left, everyone wanted to know whom he was. He did not look like the person Desiree had described that she had been dating. Desiree said,

"Oh, he's just a friend of my neighbors."

Desiree's sister, Katy could not help herself,

"Sure he is" and laughed. After her family left, Joe, whom she was casually dating, showed up. The party was long over and Desiree was over him too.

Zach made an appointment to have his haircut a few days later. He would periodically stop by unexpectedly, just to say hi. Occasionally, he would ask if Desiree would like to go and have a drink. She explained that she did not go out with married men. Toward the end of that summer, Zach called and seemed so happy,

"Guess what? I filed today, would you have dinner with me tomorrow?"

"Zach I'd love to, but you have a long road ahead of you. I've been down that road and I don't want to go down it again." He said he understood.

He continued to come in for his haircuts, and one night when Desiree called him to her chair,

"Just a moment I need to go out to my truck."

Denise had stopped by an hour before his appointment and asked if she could take Jake home. She wanted Nicky to have someone to play with, and she could use the break, so off he went.

Zach came in carrying a thermos and two glasses. He said, "

37

If you won't go out with me for a drink, I thought I would bring one to you." The thermos was full of amaretto stone sours, the only drink she drank at the time. As she was not much of a drinker, so it had to be sweet. How did he know? Her neighbor was at it again. At that moment, Desiree decided she had to date this man.

"Boy, you just don't give up, do you?"

"I am very tenacious," he replied.

"You're working, going through a divorce and running back and forth to Wisconsin, how are you going to do this?"

"I am a good juggler. You'll see." If that was a red flag waving, Desiree did not see it. She thought his wife must be crazy for letting this one go.

Desiree had believed, up to that point, that it was not a good idea to date someone who had not been divorced for at least two years, but maybe the good ones were already taken by then. She was not going to miss this opportunity, not this time.

She had turned down another client who had asked her out during his divorce and she watched him go from one girl to another and thought at the time, she had made the right decision. Who knows, maybe she should bend some of her rules and just roll with the flow. Zach was creative and very romantic, doing all of the little things and he seemed to pay attention to minute details. He would drop off small things that he heard her mention she needed. H e always asked if she was taking her vitamins, who does that? Zach brought her flowers she always had flowers.

Desiree pulled up to the parking lot of the hospital where she did her power walking and Zach's truck was there. The hospital was across from an old vacant building that was across the side street from the gym where she worked out. He wanted to surprise her. They power walked together, and even though he could walk circles around her, and did not mind telling her so, she was hooked.

Another day while she was walking and as she came around to the third and final mile, an older man remarked,

"Boy someone sure likes you. I saw flowers on your car." When Desiree got closer to the car, she realized that, sure enough, on her windshield there was a beautiful bouquet of colorful flowers. This became a regular occurrence.

Almost every evening they would sit on the glider, on Desiree's patio or, as he called it, her "veranda," with music playing in the background and talk for hours. He commented,

"I've never been this relaxed in my life; it's so peaceful when I am with you."

He spoke about how he had always wanted to be a millionaire, but it had never happened. He grew up in an affluent town but his dad worked three jobs so they could live there. He envied the friends he grew up with; one was the son of a man who owned two high-rise buildings, and had left the family millions of dollars.

Another friend's family owned trucking companies and another was the son of a doctor, and he became one as well. He was determined not to be like his father. Desiree had the impression he always felt inferior to his friends and could not seem to rise to their level.

During one of their many conversations Zach told Desiree that he had been everywhere during his marriage and did not want to go anywhere else, especially Mexico. Mexico he said "was simply a ghetto." Desiree asked if that meant that he would not take her anywhere and he said,

"No. I promise I will take you somewhere."

He came every night, had dinner with Jake and Desiree and usually cooked. She just could not believe her luck. He was handsome, thoughtful, romantic, and very well spoken, not to mention the most charming man she had ever met.

Once again, Desiree was wondering if Sheila had lost leave of her senses and was sure, she would regret the day she let him go. He told Desiree that he had worked a lot during his marriage, and by the time, he realized there was a problem; it was too late.

She had been working on her class reunion and her high school sweetheart was on the committee. Before he knew it, their meetings went from their house to going out to planning it; he was the last to know.

He tried to put the marriage back together but she told him it was too late; she did not love him anymore. One night, Zach confided in Desiree that when Sheila walked out for the last time he had told her it would be all business from that point. She turned to him and said, "Zach, there is more to life than money" and was gone.

She could see that he had regrets but was ready to move on. He decided that it would be best if he took a year off. He needed to focus on getting all of his "ducks in a row" and getting through his divorce. He felt his work would suffer if he were not concentrating.

After Sheila left the house for good, Zach invited Jake and Desiree over for dinner. He had obviously spent all day cleaning and removing anything that was Sheila's from the house. That was so thoughtful and unlike a man to think of that; she was impressed.

He had a nice home and Desiree felt very comfortable there. He had done a lot of the work himself. There was a hot tub built in the floor of the sunroom. There were sliding glass doors everywhere, overlooking a beautiful five-acre property. He had made it look like a golf course, complete with a pond and hundreds of trees; not to mention, the food was great. Desi brought flowers. What he had did not impress her but his creative ability and simple nature certainly did.

Chapter 10

Zach and Desiree were a few months into their relationship. One night, they were thinking about where they were going for the evening when he offhandedly suggested that the jeans she was wearing did nothing for her. This hurt Desiree's feelings. She noticed some moodiness but he was going through a lot so she chalked it up to that. There were times when they were watching TV after dinner and his cell phone would ring. He would pick it up, look at caller id, and lay it back down. Desiree would ask,

"Are you going to answer that?" However, he would just say,

"I don't feel like talking on the phone." She had no reason to be suspicious, after all, he was at her house every night, and some people are just like that. He told Desiree what he meant by "getting his ducks all in a row." He was emptying bank accounts, getting paper work together, and preparing for his divorce.

He let his home and property go and there were weeds as tall as Desiree was everywhere. She came over one day and the medicine cabinet had been pulled from the wall in the guest bathroom, leaving a gaping hole.

Another day Zach asked if she had any strips of cotton at the salon that he could have. She gave him some, only to find out that he had soaked them with the urine that deer hunters use and hung them from the ceiling fans. He took a water hose and sprayed down the basement to make it appear that it leaked.

He was doing this so that when the realtors came to appraise the house, they would give it a low appraisal and he would then offer Sheila half.

Desiree rationalized; after all, he had put all of this work in to a home for her. She cheated on him and left him for someone else. Even though, at the time, she thought it was a little extreme, but he was right, Sheila had hurt him enough.

He succeeded in justifying it to her even though it was a little overboard. He had also mentioned that she was on drugs and had even been selling them. As Desiree was anti-drug, his anger made sense to her; they could have lost everything if she had been caught.

One morning he called to say he was going to go to the police department to file a report. He told her Sheila apparently thought he was in Wisconsin and had come to the house during the night.

As she was making her way to the basement, he had jumped up and made her leave.

"What was she looking for?" Desiree asked.

"She was looking for the carpet cleaning machine."

"She came in the middle of the night to steal a carpet cleaning machine?" Desiree thought this was crazy, but once again, it was none of her business. It was between them.

Zach had been on different pills for anxiety. Desiree assumed it was due to his divorce. He was not able to perform sexually at all for the first six months they were together. He never spoke about it and always tried to make sure that she was happy.

That part of their life was very frustrating for her and eventually the problem took care of itself; except for the times when it seemed he was in it only for himself. He would get up or roll over and go to sleep; it got much better. She thought,

'Well he has been through a lot. Maybe we can get back to normal.'

Then there were times when he would spend the night and suddenly jump out of bed, kiss her and say,

"I have to go home." He later explained his feet would start to itch so badly, he could not lie there; he had to get up and move. Sometimes he would just go out and walk, and others he would simply leave. It would take years for him to sleep through the night.

Eventually, he and Sheila came to an agreement and their divorce was finalized. Before she knew it, he was weeding the yard and putting his house back together.

At night, they would have dinner, and Desiree would notice him staring. With questioning eyes, she would ask,

"What?"

"Have I told you today how beautiful I think you are?" and he would flash his lovely smile. She felt like a schoolgirl once again.

Desiree began to say

"I love you" and he would respond

"You are such a sweetheart" and that would be that. She thought, 'Well he shows it in other ways.' It would be five years before he told her he loved her.

He often went to Wisconsin. Sheila's family had a cottage up there, and while he could no longer go there, his close friends, Benny and Mae, who had taken his side during the divorce, had a place up there and he would visit them.

When Desiree could, they would go up there on weekends, sometimes staying with them, and at others, staying in a motel. Never the less they always had fun.

Sometimes he would go hunting and fishing with friends. That was okay with her because she had her family, friends, and her business to take care of. That was another reason for Desiree to feel good, they were both independent and did not need to be together twenty-four-seven.

Chapter 11

The year 2000 was wonderful and tragic.

Reagan came to see Desiree on her forty-fourth birthday and seemed to be in a good mood, at least when he first got there. He smiled that 'cat swallowed the canary smile' as he walked through the salon door. She was expecting him, as he wanted a haircut. Desiree had become a hairdresser back in 1981. He was up to something and he handed her a card and a gift. "Happy Birthday" he smiled.

She opened the card first and it read, 'Guys are like panty hose, when you finally find a good one...' she opened it not knowing what to expect, and it read in large letters'...IT RUNS!!!!!!'

They laughed; he knew her better than she knew herself. Desiree opened the gift. It was a blown glass oil candle in the shape of a swan. He was so excited, and since there were no other clients there, he begged her to go to her apartment because he wanted to see what it looked like lit up; so they did.

They came back to the salon and their brother, Will called to wish her 'Happy Birthday'. Reagan went into a rage when he found out Desiree was speaking to Will and began screaming at him over the phone. Apparently, he was upset because Will refused to allow him to come up to Wisconsin and visit. Reagan felt he needed to get away as he was having a hard time because of the divorce. It appeared he was not well, was losing weight, and was no longer the hunky, husky guy they all knew and loved. When she hung up the phone, Desiree tried to explain to Reagan that what he had just done did not help the situation. Then he became angry with her and she did not realize how deeply hurt he was.

In February 2000, and 6 months in to their relationship her brother Reagan, passed away. During this time, Zach proved to Desiree that he would always be there for her. He suggested where to take Reagan, and they did. She needed him to lean on. This is what Desiree had feared for years. She was so distraught she could barely breathe, much less think. Although they had a few rough times, he was always there when it counted.

Nine days later, in February 2000 after complaining of vomiting blood, and Grace accusing him of exaggerating the amount, Reagan was hospitalized. He went into a coma after they gave him a sedative to calm him.

The doctors believed he was nothing more than a drug addict. He was not using drugs at the time but the damage they had done was obvious. The truth was his liver was failing. As the liver is the control center for your brain, the doctor had later explained, when it malfunctions, your behavior becomes erratic. That was the reason given for administering the sedative. The sedative began to collect in his liver simply because it could not dispel it and it put him into a coma.

He passed away at the young age of 41. Desiree was devastated, to say the least. Reagan's death hit her harder than anything she had experienced thus far. She was no longer afraid to die. If her beloved brother had to leave, when it was her time to go, she could do it as well. Watching him suffer was tougher on her she felt than going herself.

While Desiree lost Reagan and loved him dearly, she had three terrific boys, a loving relationship with Zach and her first grandchild was born. In April Christian Michael was born, all ten pounds, six ounces of him.

Desiree was peering through the glass, looking at this miracle in her life and realized what the circle of life means, and how precious it is. Yes, God had taken her brother and Desiree did not think she would recover from his loss, but he had blessed her with Christian. While she still had, her memories of those that were dearest to her, Christian gave Desiree a reason to continue. He was healthy and his mother, Cassie had gone through a difficult labor, only to find out she would need to have a cesarean.

Desiree raised Jason and Jett and they were fine, young men. She had a long way to go with Jake; he was only eight when Christian was born. He was a great little boy and she knew he would make his brothers as proud as she was of them. She was indeed, blessed. All she had to do was love him; the rearing was someone else's responsibility. Desiree felt so lucky.

Grace was heartbroken after Reagan's death. Six months had passed when she had a series of strokes that left her paralyzed on her right side. True to form, Zach was right there, bringing her flowers and standing at her bedside when Desiree walked through the door. Yes, Desiree loved him and he kept repeatedly proving that, even though he did not say it, he loved her too.

As always, Katy was right there. Now Desiree knew why she had become a nurse, she loved taking care of the people she loved. She went home for Christmas to be with her family, promising to come back, and she did. However, she needed a break.

On Christmas Eve, Desiree went up to the hospital and spent the night with Grace and they opened gifts Christmas morning. Jake had gone to his dad's and she wanted her to have a good Christmas.

Not long after the holiday, they released her from the hospital and sent her to another, farther away. They had a rehabilitation floor and she stayed there for six weeks. Katy came back and did as much as she could to make their Mom comfortable. She was making sure she had the best care possible.

Zach never questioned her absences during this time, fully understanding once again, that she was needed somewhere else.

Katy took their mom back to Tennessee so she could take care of her. At the same time, she was torn, as she wanted to be with her family. Before Grace left, she told Braden he could continue to live in her house as long as he took care of his girls. He did not have to pay rent as long as he paid the electric and phone bills.

In the meantime, Braden's girls became wards of the state. Their mother had abandoned them, and Desiree was sure they felt abandoned once again. The girls made accusations of abuse at the hands of their father. With all they were going through as a family, this was the last thing they needed. The fear Grace always had, had indeed come true.

Braden struggled with his alcoholism and was so used to their Mom being there that he did not fare well. Desiree had become Grace's power of attorney. She began receiving double bills for everything. Braden came to the hospital and borrowed money from her to buy groceries.

Chapter 12

Desiree drove to her mom's to check on her house and found it in a shambles. Televisions were missing as well as the gas grill and many other things. Braden had taken everything of any value and pawned them. Desiree left him a note explaining that he needed to get all of his things out of the house. She was going to get it ready for when Mom came home. She waited about a week and then changed the locks.

Zach and Desiree remodeled every room in her house, making it look almost new. Just another of many reasons she loved him. Zach volunteered to do the work and did not except payment for the job. While tirelessly working one day Zach mentioned that when he went to Al's for a get together, (that Desiree had not been invited to attend) Sheila had been there.

"I had no idea she was coming and when I looked over toward the deck she was sitting there. Later, she and her brother had gone in the house and I needed to use the restroom, and went inside. I walked up to her and reached out my hand,

"I wish you the best, good-luck." She went ballistic. She was screaming while attacking me. She said, "I hate you, you son-of-a-bitch."

I was looking around; the room was full of people. I have never seen her act that way before. I don't know what her problem was."

"Maybe she still loves you, there is a fine line between love and hate, you know." "She has tried to come back, but it's too late."

They dropped the subject, tiring of that conversation and the hours they had put in; they called it quits and went home.

Braden was unemployed, as the University had fired him after they found him in possession of a prescription pad. He did not have a driving license, because of his four or five D.U.I.s. He was now jobless, homeless and on foot.

Afterwards he threatened to kill Desiree for causing so much trouble for him. Her sisters called and told her,

"If he comes to your door, no matter what; do not let him in."

At the time, Desiree was not aware of the threats but she trusted them and began to watch her back. In no time at all, and after being thrown out of every place he went, Braden called crying and asking for help. They sent him to rehab where he lived for over two years.

Katy felt after a year of rehabilitation Mom might be ready to come home. She wanted to stay with her for a couple of weeks so her transition would be easier. The damage from the stroke had been extensive. When Katy brought her home, Mom was unable to control her emotions and was afraid to stay.

Katy needed a break, and while they struggled with what to do, she decided to take Grace back with her. Desiree visited one or two weekends a month to spend time with her Mom, hoping to give Katy a much-needed break. Katy had such a routine that she found it difficult to take a break. She knew Grace's schedule better than anyone did and, what her needs were. From time to time, Desiree would bring their Mom home for three or four weeks so Katy would have some precious time to herself. Desiree cherished those stays and, although Grace was sicker than she had ever seen her, they laughed and cried. Desiree enjoyed her more than she ever had. During these visits, Brianna and Raquel took their turn having her with them as well.

Grace was ready to have surgery on her carotid arteries and went in for her pre-surgery testing. Once again, Desiree left for Tennessee knowing that this was a risky surgery and she wanted to be there however, by the time Desiree got there, she could tell by the look on Katy's face that something was wrong.

She motioned for Desiree to meet her upstairs. The surgery had been cancelled. The x-rays showed tumors on her lungs and once again, their lives changed drastically. Grace was later diagnosed with colon cancer, which had spread to her lungs and liver. They gave her up to three years to live. She, through the unbelievable will she possessed, made every one of them. Through the love and care her sister, Katy had for those that she loved, she saw that she was comfortable and Desiree believed those were the best days of her life.

The stress began taking its toll on everyone, especially Katy and including Desiree. She was 47 years old; the age their Dad was when he died of a heart attack. Suddenly, after coming back from a visit with her Mom, and spending time with her niece, she laid down on the couch. She felt like she had hit a brick wall.

Zach had encouraged Desiree to take a Zanax occasionally. When she would refuse, he would say,

"Just take a half of one to calm your nerves so you can get a good night's sleep." He was always taking something. It was a pill for his stomach, something for his sinuses and Zanax, so he could sleep.

"I don't like to take medicine."

"It won't hurt you to take one; that is what it's for." She would rarely agree, and he would just shake his head.

She had been having frequent, pounding headaches and she just could not get her strength up. Desiree went to the local Wal-mart and sat down at the blood pressure machine. As the cuff tightened, Desiree wondered what she was doing there.

She had always been healthy but she sat there anyway. The results stunned her: 200 over 110. Desiree called Zach; he came over and immediately called his friend, Dr. Daniel. He advised him to give her an aspirin and dial 911. Zach gave Desiree an aspirin and against Dr. Daniel's urging, decided to drive her to the hospital.

They took her blood pressure and it had not gone down. They took her in right away, placed a nitro patch on her chest, and did an EKG. Gradually her blood pressure came down, and after getting the results from the EKG showing that she had not had a heart attack, they released her.

Desiree began checking her blood pressure several times a day, while Dr. Daniel kept trying different medications to bring it down. After one more visit to the hospital, Dr. Daniel suggested that she only check her blood pressure once in the morning and at night. He thought Desiree was checking it too often and that could be why it was so high. Before long, they had it under control.

She did not realize that, while she did not mourn her father's death at the age of eleven, when she turned the age he was at his death, Desiree would have the very symptoms that caused his death. It had not seemed to bother her back then; apparently, she was emotionally unable to handle it at the time, so Desiree buried it. Eventually she had to deal with it. Frankly after Reagan's passing, Desiree felt she could handle anything and was now strong enough emotionally to deal with it. She thought maybe the saying is true that 'God will not give you more than you can handle'.

In July 2002 their first baby girl, Grace Ella was born, seven pounds, six ounces. Jason and Cassie had done it again. She was perfect in every way, but of course, Desiree was not prejudiced. Since Cassie and Jason's grandmothers shared the same name, they decided it would be fitting to give it to their daughter.

Grace was staying with Desiree at the time and she drove her to the hospital. She was in a wheelchair but was always ready when anyone said, "Let's go." Desiree wheeled her down the hall that led to the beautiful babies, screaming at the top of their little lungs. Barely high enough to see, she looked through the glass as they pointed her out. Jason told her, "Grandma, her name is Grace Ella." Her eyes lit up and she smiled with delight. Grace, with no more pressures of rearing children had become a dear and loving grandmother. She was now the person she was always meant be. Following Reagan's death and their mother's stroke, it was as though their family had suddenly been cursed, and just when she thought it could not get worse; it did.

Chapter 13

It was July 27, 2002; it began as every other day. Desiree went to work around noon and just as quickly as her workday had begun, it ended with a phone call from Dan. She did not understand what he was saying, when suddenly it became clear that Jake had been involved in a serious accident. He was spending part of his summer break with his dad.

Desiree was not certain what happens when you hear bad news. It felt like everything sounded distorted and she could only make sense out of a few of the words he was saying,

She heard, concerned, hip, accident, and you need to come to the Hospital. She was hysterical. Desiree explained to her client that she had to leave, she rushed her out of the salon, locked the door, hopped in her car, and left. She scarcely remembered calling Jason and stopping by the high school where he worked to pick him up. Jason could see that she was in shock so he drove. Desiree did not recall the drive to the hospital; she only remembered rushing in to find her son.

When they arrived in the E.R., they directed Desiree to his room. When she rounded the corner, there he lay, hooked to an I.V., and bruised from head to toe. As she reached his bedside, she could see tiny cuts all over him. The nurse was administering morphine. Desiree asked if morphine was necessary. She explained that they were unsure at that point the extent of his injuries. Jake's color was poor, and he was drifting in and out of consciousness.

She left his room only long enough to try to find out what had happened, when she ran in to her brother-in-law, Rob. He had been working on the overpass on I-65 where the accident had occurred and witnessed it. He was there to make certain Jake was okay. Desiree had no idea how he knew Jake was in the van.

Apparently, a dump truck driver was watching the guys working on the overpass and did not realize traffic had slowed down for a state truck that was painting stripes on the highway. His truck rear-ended the van on the left side, as he swerved to avoid the collision. Jake was in the last seat on the left side.

Dan explained that his sister-in-law had decided to take all of the kids to Toys-R-Us, all six of them. One child had been thrown from the van, and all had injuries. After being rear-ended, the van flipped and skid across the highway causing friction and a small fire in the grass. The van was upside down and one of Rob's workers found Jake trapped inside. He extinguished the fire, and pulled Jake from the van.

Raquel, a 911 dispatcher got the call. She worked in a nearby county and they needed extra ambulances. There were seven people in the van. They needed to be transported to the hospital.

Jake had a broken hip, glass embedded in his skin from head to toe, a concussion and was bruised so severely that his blood count was extremely low. He was vomiting every fifteen minutes like clockwork. Desiree called Zach to let him know what had happened. He was busy working and could not make it. She was too distraught to argue and went back to check on Jake.

The hospital would become her home for three days. Once the nurses got Jake settled in his room and while they were sitting at his bedside, Jett came barreling in the room. He was shaking all over and when he saw Jake, he collapsed, and cried like a baby. He had gotten there in record time, and stayed until after Jake was released from the hospital.

Zach said he would not be able to make it; he was so busy with work, and was invited to a high school graduation party on Sunday.

Desiree was furious. She did not understand how he could be so thoughtful one minute, and so thoughtless the next. She chalked it up to the fact that he did not have children.

When Desiree brought Jake home, Zach insisted she bring him to his house. He cooked dinner and put Jake in the hot tub in the sunroom. He felt the bruising would dissipate quicker. Desiree soon forgot about what she had perceived to be inconsiderate behavior, and they went on. The first night Jake was home Desiree went in to tuck him in his bed.

"Mom, Uncle Reagan was there."

"I bet he was, buddy."

"I mean it Mom he was, he held the van tight so it wouldn't crush me."

He was serious and Desiree got chills. They spoke a while longer and Jett slept in his room, that night. Her clients and friends showered him with gifts, sent him cards, and she reminded him that they would need to make a list so they could send thank-you cards.

When Jett left, Jake asked if he could sleep with her, he was having nightmares. His physical wounds would take less time to heal than the memories that were slowly resurfacing about his accident would take to fade away.

There were many weeks of rehabilitation. Jake could not walk so Desiree would carry him. She carried him to the restroom, to the table for meals, to take a bath and to bed. Desiree dressed him, carried him to the car, and took him to work.

She soon borrowed a wheelchair, which helped tremendously. Zach brought a bed to the salon, and placed it in the waiting area. It lifted up so he could watch television, play video games, and it lowered when he wanted to nap.

Zach carried Jake to his truck on a regular basis to take him home and put him in his hot tub.

They had several appointments to have glass removed from his head and various other body parts. His blood count was going up, and his hip was growing new bone. The doctor explained that his hip had been crushed and his body would absorb it, and in the meantime, he was growing new bone. He said, "If that were you or I at our age, it would take us six months to progress at the rate he was healing in six weeks." Desiree reminded him to speak for himself.

Jake and Desiree were a team and they managed to get through another obstacle and went back to their life as usual. Jake was now on crutches, and back at school.

Desiree was a volunteer at a center behind the local hospital where she regularly power walked; Desiree cut hair for children who had become wards of the state. She always knew how her Mom felt about accepting help from the state and it was her way of paying back. She knew she could have very easily been there, but Grace saw to it that it never happened.

Desiree was stunned to find out that one of her nieces was at that center but she became her sponsor. She began cutting her hair, going to counseling sessions, to dinners on visiting days and holidays. Desiree brought her gifts at Christmas and gave her gift bags filled with hair products for each person on the ward. Desiree was certain it brought more joy to her than to them.

Although she was mortified to find out that her niece was where she was volunteering, it made her realize it is a small world after all.

Fall was turning into winter and Desiree realized Jake and she needed to sit down and get thank-you cards filled out. They sat down to make his list. There were nineteen people on the list and Desiree told him that he should personally fill them out, to show his appreciation.

Suddenly, he said,

"I think we are forgetting someone." She could almost see the wheels turning, as he was determined not to forget anyone.

He suddenly exclaimed,

"I know! We forgot Uncle Reagan." Without batting an eye, she jotted down his name.

"Okay buddy, here is your list, you fill them out and I will mail them for you."

"How will Uncle Reagan get his?"

"I know, the next time we see a helium balloon, we will attach it to the card and send it to heaven."

"That's a great idea."

A few days later, they stopped at Applebee's for lunch.

"Hey Mom, look!" Jake exclaimed with delight.

"What?"

"Balloons."

They took one home.

Desiree took a punch and strategically placed a whole in the corner of the envelope so it would not ruin Jake's note to Uncle Reagan. They ran the string through the hole and gently tied it.

"Put your shoes on and let's go outside."

They put on their shoes and coats and off they went. It was a dreary and cloudy day that day. Desiree kept thinking to herself, 'Couldn't we have chosen a better day.'

Jake wanted to find the perfect spot to release the balloon. He wanted to make sure it reached its destination.

When they found an open spot, he said,

"Mom, count to three."

"One...Two...Three..."

He let it go. They watched it until she could barely see it; and Desiree turned and went back inside. By the time, Desiree took her shoes, and coat off and sat down in her room; Jake came running in,

"He got it Mom, he got it!"

As Desiree came down the hall to find out what was going on she said,

"How do you know he got it?"

He grabbed her arm and began dragging her down the hall.

"You'll see, come on!"

As Desiree walked in the living room, he yelped,

"See Mom, look… the sun is shining!"

With tears filling her eyes and spilling over on to her cheeks, Desiree said,

"I see."

The sun was out only for a moment, and then disappeared once again behind the clouds.

In the meantime, Zach was in the process of selling the dry cleaners he owned with his partner, Ike. Desiree had not met Ike. She only knew him as the partner who was wealthy and owned not only the dry cleaners, but also the strip mall where it was located. Dry cleaners were becoming obsolete and no longer seemed to be a profitable business. The only perk was that it was a cash business. Zach did not speak about his business much; he was very private about the details. He mentioned that a guy had purchased it on contract. He was relieved to have gotten rid of it. It would be one less thing to worry about. Shortly after the sale, Zach called and said that the bookstore Ike owned had caught on fire and that the damage had been extensive. The bookstore was located in the strip mall that Ike also owned.

When Zach came by to get a haircut, Desiree asked what had happened. Zach said, "I don't know, they are investigating. I feel sorry for Ike; everything seems to be going wrong. "He is going through a nasty divorce and now this." As he was relaying the story, Desiree was cutting his hair while looking at him in the mirror. He had, what appeared to be red lipstick, on his mouth. She was trying to listen to him, but his voice was fading in and out; Desiree was fixated on his mouth. It was smeared vertically across his bottom lip and chin. It cannot be lipstick, she kept telling herself. Finally, he looked at her, "What's wrong?"

"You have lipstick on your mouth and chin."

Without skipping a beat, "I stopped by the trucking company, and Kaitlyn kissed me good-bye."

Kaitlyn was Keith's sister and they had known each other their entire lives. Desiree breathed a sigh of relief and reminded herself not to jump to conclusions. Zach wiped his mouth, kissed her, and left. It was not long before he came walking back through the door.

This time Desiree glanced in the mirror at Zach's reflection. He was standing there, wearing that million-dollar smile, and holding a bouquet of flowers. He busied himself with cutting the flowers and arranging them in a vase while she finished up with her client. He sat there for the longest time, not making conversation, just sitting there. From time to time, he did this but Desiree did not understand it. He always had to be moving. Maybe he wanted to make sure she was not upset about Kaitlyn's lipstick ending up sideways on his mouth and chin. Desiree kept visualizing it repeatedly in her mind, thinking; "How does that happen with a friendly kiss?"

Before long, Zach announced the investigators believed the fire was arson and were taking entirely too long. Ike was going to have Zach rebuild the bookstore as soon as the investigators had finished and released it. After a few months, although they continued to believe it was arson, they could not prove it and closed the case. Zach was happy to have a job. It was too bad that this had to happen so he could get work.

Chapter 14

On Christmas morning 2002, Zach spent the night so he would be there for their early morning gift opening. Just like when Desiree was a young girl, and when Jason and Jett would wake her at about 4 am to open their presents, and after saying "no" a few times to build up the suspense, she would relent.

Later in the morning and much to her surprise, Zach asked Desiree if she would like to go to his mom's for breakfast. She had met his sister Trish once before, but during the three and a half years they had been together; she had never met his mother. Of course, Desiree agreed and off they went.

She met them at the door; she was a very short, petite woman with beautiful silver hair. Just as Desiree had expected, she was a pretty and classy woman, and contrary to her looks, she was very down to earth.

The first thing she said after Zach introduced them and after a very welcome hug, was "I have been asking Zach for a long time to please bring you over so that I could meet you."

"That is funny. I asked that as well" Desiree responded.

They had a great conversation during breakfast and exchanged small gifts afterward. Neither of them had planned this meeting. She had most likely searched everywhere until she found something to give her. Desiree thought, maybe she was like her and kept extra things in a closet just for these occasions. She was delighted they had met and felt that bigger things in their relationship were yet to come.

After many months of pain and discomfort, Desiree was scheduled for a complete hysterectomy and once again, Zach was there.

The surgery went well and although she was in tremendous pain, Desiree came home. She spent much of the first week in her recliner; it even became her bed at night. Zach was there to make sure she had her medication, and because Desiree had drainage tubes, he emptied those as well. He never ceased to amaze her.

However, after a few days, he was back to work and stopping by, but by this time, his sudden appearances and disappearances had become normal. She was almost used to it. Desiree spent a lot of time in bed watching television, not wanting to move around anymore than she had to. As she was surfing the channels Desiree heard the door open, "Baby, where are you? I'm here."

As Zach sat on the edge of her bed he handed Desiree a few chocolate goodies, "You lazy thing, why are you still in bed?"

Desiree held her pillow against her abdomen, waiting for him to make her laugh. That pillow had become her best friend. "Hi honey, where have you been?"

"Just running around. Hey, did I tell you the guy that bought the dry cleaners was found dead?"

"No! What happened?"

"They found him in the parking lot. He'd been shot."

"That's awful, I can't believe it."

"Oh well, those things happen."

"Zach! He was probably murdered." He eased off the bed, stood to leave, and as he walked toward the door, said,

"What can you do?"

Desiree just shook her head. 'Sometimes' she thought, 'he can be so sensitive and at others, he does not even seem human.' She supposed he had a lot on his mind.

In 2003, after several "We need a break" months and her surgery, Zach's behavior became peculiar and he was becoming more and more distant. Zach was impulsive and always changing his plans.

"You know me; I could say I am doing one thing and end up doing something totally different, my day changes by the minute."

He told Desiree he was tired of being a contractor, that he was burnt out and just did not want do it anymore.

Not long after that, his distance became quite apparent. As they often did, Zach and Desiree were having dinner at a restaurant. Before they were even served he said, "Sweetie, I have been hired by Lowes." You might say that Desiree was a bit surprised. What would he tell his friends as it seemed a little beneath him after working on his own so long.

On Friday evening, they went to Jake's indoor soccer game and, not only did he seem distant, but very irritated as well. It seemed that everything she said upset him and Desiree began to feel she was walking on eggshells. It was not the first time; and it would not be the last. They were supposed to go out with her friends after the game, but he said he did not feel like it and dropped her off at her apartment. The following morning while Desiree was at work, Zach called and in an agitated and firm voice said, "We need to talk." He seemed angry and Desiree could not imagine what she had done now. She told him what time she would be home so he could come over. He called shortly after Desiree came home and did not sound as though his mood had improved much from the previous evening.

"Sweetie, I won't be coming over today, I have a horrible headache."

"I have had enough, Zach. I'm going to make this easy on you, if you are trying to end our relationship and you want it to be over, just say so."

He replied, "Sweetie, I am moving to Wisconsin. I put in for a transfer to the Lowes in Wisconsin."

The year prior, he had bought 80 acres and had built a pole barn on the property.

Desiree had fond memories of going up there on the weekends to help him. When it was just a concrete slab and only the rafters were up, they would have campfires and sleep in the camper. One day he came and said,

"Hurry baby, you have five minutes to take a shower." With the look of bewilderment crossing her face, Desiree went to see what he had done. There was a drain in the middle of the concrete slab, and over it, he had concocted a makeshift shower. He had taken a water hose and tossed it over a rafter, and attached a showerhead to it. He had also heated water, put it in a five-gallon cooler, and placed a pump in it. He then attached the other end of the hose to the pump. For his final touch, he took a blue plastic tarp and hung it in a square around his invention, from the rafters, thus she had a shower. Zach was an eagle scout and he was ingenious in the manner in which he could take nothing and make something out of it. Just one of the many reasons, Desiree loved him. However, he could not build a toilet, so she would have to pee in the woods.

Zach built a three-bedroom cabin inside of the pole barn. The garage was facing the front of the property, while the cabin faced the back, overlooking the woods. Zach had made special covers for each window and covered them every time he left. Desiree assumed he was afraid of break-ins if when was gone.

It was supposed to be a place for him and his friends to stay while hunting and fishing and for them to spend their weekends away. Now it looked as though it was going to be home, at least for him. After four years, just like that, he announced he was leaving.

Desiree began to journal her feelings. After all, Oprah says it is a good idea; it can't hurt. Every time she would give her sons advice, they would laugh and say,

"Mom have you been watching Oprah again?"

She could not let go that easily and suggested they continue their relationship and commute.

"I don't see why we couldn't do that. I'll talk to you about it later," and they hung up.

The following day he went to Benchwarmers and gave Denise everything Desiree had left at his house, along with the keys to her house. It took her three days to get up the nerve to bring them over. Denise explained to her that Zach said that it was not over but that he was going to be busy for a while.

Three weeks went by and during that time, Desiree became severely depressed. Then, unexpectedly he called to see how she was doing. They spoke for a while, and he mentioned that he would be leaving for Wisconsin on Saturday and coming back on Wednesday. He had arranged his days off for the next two weeks together so he could go for five days.

While watching television on Sunday, her phone rang; she was surprised to hear Zach's voice, "What's going on?"

"Nothing how's the weather up there?"

"Oh I didn't go; the truck needed brakes, so I stayed here to work on them."

He asked if she wanted to go out for breakfast the next morning and after accepting his offer, they said good-bye. He picked Desiree up and they were back together as though nothing had happened, and as if they had never been apart.

Everything seemed fine but while they were together one evening having dinner, in his usual fashion, he blurted out the fact that his transfer had gone through and he would soon be leaving. With tears welling up in her eyes, he explained,

"Sweetie, I am not leaving you, I am just moving to Wisconsin."

The only words Desiree heard were not from Zach, but from her father,

"I am not leaving you, I just died." She began to weep. Desiree finally pulled herself together and quipped,

"Boy, you really know how to ruin a good meal."

In an attempt to relieve some of his guilt, she went on to say,

"Everyone should follow their dream and I will be here to help you realize yours." They began working on his house to get it ready to sell. While Zach was working, Desiree would go over and pack boxes.

One day she was standing in the garage and Zach was making small talk. Desiree was staring behind him and he said, "What's wrong?"

"Where'd that room come from?" He turned around and looked as though he had not noticed there was a room there.

"Oh that; it's a safe room. If there were a storm, you would be safe in there. It is fireproof as well. Do you want to see it?"

It was a small room with no windows; he had albums and a few other things in there. She did not see anything of great value. Desiree could not help wandering though; if that was where Sheila was going the night, he caught her. He explained that he had put a heavy piece of plywood paneling in front of the door but never said why and Desiree never asked.

Chapter 15

The day came for Zach to leave. His best friend, Al, and Desiree were there to pack up his big tractor-trailer with as many possessions as they could safely load on to it. When they were finished, she walked over and put her hands on his waist,

"Before you go,"

"Before I go, what?" with anticipation in his eyes.

Desiree asked,

"Do you wanna dance?"

He smiled,

"Sweetie, sweetie, sweetie... I am dancing."

He jumped in his truck after shaking Al's hand and kissing Desiree good-bye, and then drove away. He did not look back. Al turned to her and said, "This must be killing you, it's hard even for me to see him go."

The day dragged slowly. She did not cry; Desiree knew everything would be fine. Zach called at bedtime to let her know he had got there safely, and to say goodnight. He was exhausted and hung up. After tossing and turning, and as she was finally drifting, off to sleep, the phone rang. Desiree glanced at the clock; it was just after midnight. Who in their right mind is calling this late? As she picked up the phone, she noticed it was a blocked call. "Hello." No answer, but she could hear noise in the background. After about thirty seconds, they hung up.

This had never happened before. The first thing Desiree thought was 'Zach left today, and then I get a blocked call.' It was her first

– but it would not be her last. A pattern began developing. She began to make a log of the date and the time these phone calls came in. Desiree did not mention this to Zach; after all, it might be just a coincidence.

The calls continued and usually came right before or right after the weekend but always on Thursday mornings. During August, September, and October, Desiree spent many of her weekends with Zach. She went there when Jake spent time with his dad.

Zach did not socialize much for the first few months he was up there. He would call Desiree on his lunch breaks, saying that he was sitting in his truck, eating. He did not like working at Lowes but he had made the choice to go there and she assumed it was worth the sacrifice. It was Thursday evening and Desiree was looking forward to seeing Zach. Her phone rang,

"Hi sweetie, I need a favor."

Always happy to hear from him,

"Hi, babe I was just thinking of you, what's up?"

"I'm looking for some papers and I need you to go to the house and get them."

"Where are they?"

"In my office, call me when you get there."

It was getting late and it was a good thing his house was nearby, as it would only take a couple of minutes. Desiree called him as she was turning into the driveway.

"Sweetie, go to my office. I am looking for my plot of survey. Look in the top drawer on the right hand side of my desk."

She searched his entire desk but could not find the paper.

"Trust me; it is not in your desk."

"Okay babe, do you see the built-in bookshelf behind you, to your left."

Desiree turned to her left and behind her.

"Yes, I'm looking at it." She had seen it many times before.

"Do you see the wall below the shelves?"

"Yes."

"Go over there and push up on it."

"Why?"

"You ask too many questions. It is a false wall. There's a safe behind it."

Maybe Zach was right, maybe she had been living under a rock. Desiree wore her heart on her sleeve and was an open book, while Zach seemed to hide everything. She struggled, pulled, pushed, and tugged until she finally managed to move the wall upward. Sure enough, there was a safe with a combination lock.

"Now what?"

"Put it in the car and bring it with you tomorrow."

Wondering why he did not just give her the combination to open it, she replied,

"I can't lift this thing, it's too heavy." There was a pause and she thought he was trying to remember the combination.

"I'll call Will next door and have him load it in your car. Whatever you do, do not leave your car unlocked. There's money in there."

It was a Friday in early November, and Desiree was finishing work early so she could get on the road when the salon phone rang; a blocked call and no one spoke. Then silence. She did not go back home before she left. She would have probably been a bit more disturbed to see she had a blocked call at her apartment at the same time as well.

Desiree had her car packed so she could head up to Wisconsin early; it is a four-hour drive up there, and she wanted to spend as much time with Zach as she could. She was always anxious to see him; Sunday always came quickly and it would be time to leave.

At this point, their arrangement was working out well; Desiree was certain everything was going to be fine. Despite the fact that her clients felt otherwise, she happily continued to make these trips. She called Zach on her way,

"Hi babe, do you need anything?"

She should have known what his reply would be by now,

"A bag of money."

She always got that answer. Somehow, she was always surprised when he said it. Zach was so down to earth and such a simple person, he must be joking. Desiree laughed, "I will be there soon."

He greeted her with open arms as he always did. He helped bring everything in, including his safe. He did not open it; he just took it to his office. He was preparing dinner for two, complete with candles, as always. It was a lazy weekend, and they spent much of it at the cabin. He catered to her as usual with a head rub, back and foot massage, and anything else he felt would help Desiree relax. Zach always kept a container of lotion on the floor, next to his bed just for those occasions. Other than their walks around his property and their fireside chats, they spent much of their time at the cabin. They were catching up on everything that was going on.

While they spoke several times a day everyday on the phone, they tried to keep their conversations short.

"Hey babe," Desiree asked,

"Whatever happened to Ike, you never talk about him. Have you spoken to him lately?"

He appeared to be agitated,

"No, the son of a bitch owes money for the taxes on the dry cleaners. He will not return my calls. I am going to take the papers to Indiana when I come down and drop them off at the bookstore. There seemed to be more to the story but Desiree let it go. She did not want to ruin the weekend.

Zach went outside to take the comforter off the line; he liked to air his linens out and loved the smell after they had been in the fresh air. His phone rang and she thought nothing of answering it,

"Hello" a girl's voice,

"Is Zach there?"

"Yes he is."

"Can I speak to him please?"

"Sure, hold on."

Zach was walking through the door, his arms full of comforter, and Desiree held the phone toward him. The look on her face betrayed her, and he asked,

"Who is it?" She shrugged and he laid the blanket down to take the call.

"Hello" and from there on, the weekend fell apart. His face turned pale and then red and he said, "mmmhm, no, yes, mmmhm, yes, no, no, I live here now. No,"

His voice became very soft and soothing and he said,

"I will tell you what, when I come down we'll get together and discuss it, okay?" He then said goodbye, and hung up the phone.

Desiree stood as if frozen and staring in to space, not knowing what had just transpired. Zach snuck up behind her, wrapped his arms around her waist, and as he nibbled on her ear he whispered,

"That was a friend of Matthew and Lisa's. He moved away,

"She's from Hammond, and she wants me to do some work for her."

"What kind of work?"

"Oh, she has a place next to her parents and she wants them connected somehow." Together they made the bed and the rest of the evening was uneventful and very quiet.

Chapter 16

Zach always had a spiral notebook lying on the coffee table; it contained the phone numbers of his friends and business contacts.

It was early November in 2003 and her weekend to see Zach. Friday night before bed, he went in to take a shower and for the first time, Desiree opened it. On the first page, there were many numbers, including hers, and just above her name was a Hammond phone number. It was for a girl named Tara. She wrote the name and number down, put it in her purse, and never mentioned the incident before she left. Desiree completely forgot about the safe, the false wall, and the secrets. She now focused on the blocked calls at home and the call from the girl from Hammond.

Desiree could not get this call off her mind and when she got home, she decided to call Denise just to get someone else's opinion. Denise told her Matthew and Lisa was trying to get Zach to go out with a friend of Lisa's she had gone to school with. It was just before they had met. She had overheard the conversation at the bar and Zach had not been interested.

Everything about that conversation with the girl from Hammond was strange; his one-word answers, together with the fact there was no mention of the job she wanted him to do. During the call, his face changed color. All of this gave Desiree a bad feeling in her gut for days.

She thought back to before he moved, how he would get calls, and after looking at caller id, he would not answer certain ones. She thought it through and could not hold back any longer. When Zach called to say good night, Desiree told him,

"I just cannot seem to get that call out of my head."

That soft, soothing voice came back and said,

"I told you she is a friend of Matthew and Lisa and she needs some work done."

"Why wasn't there any mention of the job, just one word answers? That call made me very uncomfortable."

"Oh, you are too suspicious, jealous, and you think too much."

Then she let it go, but it was around that time Desiree decided to become an amateur private investigator. Two weeks later her friend, Mariah came in to have her usual highlights and haircut. As always, they were telling each other their personal problems and, as in most cases, the subject was men.

Desiree told her the latest story and mentioned the girl's name was Tara. Mariah said,

"I went to high school with a Tara, Is she from Hammond?"

"Yep."

"Is her last name, Hubbard?"

"I don't know. I'll have to check."

"If it is, I don't think you have anything to worry about, she isn't Zach's type. I think she lives on Lemon Street on the border of Highland."

They then changed the subject, and as she was her last client of the day, Desiree went home. She pulled out her phone book and looked up Hubbard on Lemon Street. Sure enough there it was. She jotted down the address and put it away as it would have to wait until tomorrow.

The next day Desiree nervously took a ride to the address on Lemon Street and as she pulled in the driveway, the first thing she noticed was there were two places, just as Zach had said; a house with a garage, and what appeared to be a new addition above the garage. It was already connected by a new breezeway. Why was he lying?

When Zach called, as he always did, she asked him,

"What is the name of the girl that called you when I was up there?"

"Tara."

"Is Tara's last name, Hubbard?"

"Yes."

"One of my clients knows her; does she live on Lemon Street?"

"I don't know"

"You've never been to her house?"

"No, you need to relax. You ask too many questions, and you need to stay out of my business."

Well, Desiree thought 'I cannot accuse him because I do not know.' Maybe she was jumping to conclusions she let it go. Less than a week later Zach called early, to say good night. He was tired, sounded angry, and said he just did not feel like talking.

She prepared dinner for Jake and herself but Zach's mood bothered her. When they were finished eating, Desiree gave him a call to see if he was all right. They spoke for a few minutes and he said he did not know what was wrong with his phone. It had been on the charger all day but the battery was still dying.

About that time, she received a call but because Zach's phone was dying, she decided not to take it; she would just call them back. She did not recognize the number but she called back and it went to a voice mail. A female voice said,

"I am sorry I could not take your call, please leave a brief message and I will get back to you." She left a message but whoever it was never returned her call.

A few weeks passed, and Desiree went back to Wisconsin. Everything seemed normal, as though he had forgotten the whole incident. Zach went to take a shower after dinner. She noticed he had left his phone bill lying on the dining table. It was as if it was on display, so of course, Desiree accepted the invitation and looked at it.

There was a call to a Hammond number that lasted 15 minutes. The date of the call was the same evening Zach had called early to say goodnight. She thought that must have been the reason the battery was dying on his phone. As she thought about it, Desiree remembered, it was that same night another call came in while they were talking. Zach only came home once during the following three months. It was for one overnight stay, and he said he would be bringing Dave with him. Dave was a longtime friend from Wisconsin. He needed help loading and pulling his tractor because he said his truck could not handle it.

He explained he would not see her because he was taking Dave out with his friends. This was the first time he had come home and had not come over.

Zach called the next morning and told her he was leaving to go back up North and would stop by for a minute. He had sold her tanning bed from the salon to a girl he worked with at Lowe's and would drop off her money. He was at her house for no more than five minutes before he left. Within five minutes her phone rang, it was a blocked call. She picked it up and decided not to say anything. For the first time, a female said,

"Hello". Desiree just held the phone and then hung up. The phone rang again and she just let it ring.

Late that evening Zach called to let her know he had just got home.

"What happened?" she asked.

He said,

"Well I didn't leave right away. I had to put the storm windows in the house and we had to drive slowly because of the tractor."

Desiree called the police and told them she was getting harassing calls and wanted a trace put on her phone. They told her they could do that free of charge for 30 days. The man gave Desiree the number to report the dates and times of each call.

The calls stopped and after a few weeks, she told Zach,

"Don't you think it's odd that all of a sudden, after Matthew and Lisa's friend called up there, and other than the one night you came home, those blocked calls have stopped?" He blew that question off and changed the subject. Even though she did not have any proof that anything was going on, Desiree was suspicious.

Zach seemed to be getting used to being in Wisconsin and becoming more comfortable with his job. He even bought a Santa hat to wear to work, which was totally out of character. He was usually just an observer of activities and not a participant. Zach always kept a low profile and Desiree began to notice he always had to sit with his back to the wall. Zach seemed uncomfortable unless he faced the door. She thought that maybe being up there, away from his old life, was doing him good and maybe now he could relax.

Over the next two months, she received two blocked calls, one in December, and one in January but they were different from the others. They were in the middle of the night and did not follow the pattern of the other calls. The second call was at 2 am on a Thursday morning.

The phone rang; Desiree picked it up and said "Hello." The caller just held the phone. She heard a sharp beep and the phone went dead. She had heard that beep before, but where. She decided Zach was right, she was going to drive herself crazy and should just stop letting these things bother her. She went back to bed.

Desiree did not mention these calls to Zach because he would surely think she had gone nuts. A few days passed and during one of their phone conversations he asked,

"Have you been getting those calls again?"

She was surprised he asked and Desiree replied,

"Yes, why?"

"Because you've been acting strange, I thought you probably were. I have been racking my brain trying to figure out who's been doing this and the only thing I could come up with was Sheila."

She pondered this momentarily. That did not make sense to her. Zach also commented on Sheila's boyfriend. "I hear her boyfriend is threatening to beat my ass. He is nothing but a little weasel."

Desiree could not wrap her brain around this.

"After four years what reason would Sheila have to call me? I was getting calls late mornings on Thursdays and she works on Thursdays, right?" Why, she thought, would her boyfriend want to beat his ass when he had been seeing his wife while they were married? It did not make sense, but not much did these days.

"Well she is off on Wednesdays and goes in late on Thursdays. I don't care what you say, I think it's her."

Later Desiree was trying to rationalize why Sheila would be calling her now; after all, she was in a happy relationship. She certainly could not understand why her boyfriend would threaten Zach. She remembered a conversation they had after about six months of dating.

"You know I am surprised Sheila has never called me."

"She would never do that, trust me. She tells everyone that she is afraid of me, isn't that strange?"

"Why would anyone be afraid of you?" He just shrugged his shoulders and ended the conversation.

The next time she went up North, Desiree looked for the phone bills. When Zach went in to take his shower, she went in his office. Desiree crossed a line she had never crossed before and, although she was feeling guilty, she would cross it many more times. She looked in the files that held his bills.

He was meticulous about keeping his bills in separate folders each month, with all of his bills stapled together. Boy, she thought, 'I wish I was this organized.' Each bill was there for every month, except December and January's phone bills were missing. 'Oh my God, did he call me to make me believe it was Sheila?'

That night, feeling uneasy, they went to bed, and cuddled while they watched television. They then turned out the lights and within minutes, Zach was sound asleep. In Wisconsin, the nightly silence is deafening, other than the coyotes howling and the noises from the other critters that roam about up there, you can hear the proverbial pin drop. She was drifting off to sleep when she heard a sharp beep;

the same beep she had heard the night she got the call at 2 am. A creepy feeling enveloped her.

Once again, another sleepless night and once again she did not say a word about it. Maybe she was crazy or thinking too much, like he always tells her. Desiree tossed and turned until she finally fell asleep. The weekend was soon over and it was time to go.

Jake and Desiree had plans for the following weekend. They were taking the train to Chicago. He loved going there to see the tall buildings and Desiree enjoyed seeing him have fun. Jake was full of anticipation and she was back to work, so they could afford to go. Thursday while at work, she decided to go home for lunch. It was walking distance and Desiree was starving. It was late afternoon and she had missed lunch so now called it dinner. As was her habit, she went to the phone, checked caller i.d. to see if anyone had called. 'That is odd, Zach called earlier, and he knows I am at work.' She picked up the phone and dialed his number. "Hello."

"Hey, you called." Silence.

"Zach, did you call me?"

"Yes."

"What did you want?"

"Nothing."

"Why did you call me at home on a Thursday, when you know I am at work?"

"I don't know."

"What is wrong with you, you are acting strange?"

"Nothing."

"You don't know why you called me at home, when I was at work?"

"No."

"Why are you giving me one word answers and why do you sound so angry?"

"I don't know, Tim is here, do you want to talk to him?"

"Sure." Tim got on the phone,

"Hey, Des."

"Hi, Tim, how are you?"

"Not bad, I stopped by to visit with Zach."

"Tell Zach I will talk to him later."

"Here's Zach."

"Hey."

"I will let you go; I hope your day gets better." 'How does he go from being wonderful to weird like that? I guess we all have bad days.' She grabbed something to eat and Jake and Desiree went back to work.

Chapter 17

In February of 2004, it was her turn to take care of him. Zach was having surgery on his knee. She was there for him when he had his gallbladder removed as well. That is what relationships are all about, being there for each other. He had told her to call and schedule it so Desiree chose her forty-eighth birthday. She knew he would be laid up for a while so she brought enough food for a couple of weeks, so once she was gone, he would have plenty to eat. She made sure it would be microwavable and easy for him to fix. After all, he was alone up there and would not have anyone to cook for him.

Desiree was there for Valentine's Day and she took notice of the fact he did not get any phone calls. This made Desiree believe her suspicions were unfounded and ridiculous. She was reassured, and forgot about it. Zach had his surgery and when he awoke in recovery, they called Desiree back to see him. She walked over to his bedside and when he looked up Desiree asked, "Do you wanna dance?"

"Sweetie, I am dancing," he gently replied.

She smiled and took his hand. As soon as they were able, she took him home. Once again, no one called, so Desiree assured herself that nothing was going on. She helped him with his showers and made sure he had breakfast, lunch and dinner and was happy to do so.

His mother called to check on him. He explained to her that Desiree was going to be there for five days, so not to worry. When he got off the phone, he said she had told him, "Boy, she sure takes good care of you," and he agreed.

There were no strange calls apart from the one from the phone company. He had not paid his last two bills. He explained to them he had lost them and would send payment in right away. Maybe she was over thinking, maybe it was just coincidence that he lost those two bills. When her mind went back to those two blocked calls, once again, Desiree became upset.

She asked Zach if he would come home with her to Indiana, as she did not believe he was ready to take care of himself just yet. He said if he went back, he would be doing the same thing there just lying around, and he did not want to do that.

He had not been back to Indiana for three months, and Desiree wanted him to come so she would not worry about him, but he flatly refused. Desiree left and after being away from him for a while, she began to think about all the strange things that had happened. Her gut feeling that something was not right came back stronger each time, so after four and a half years she decided to end the relationship.

It was never easy; she missed him as though she had lost a limb. Desiree was depressed and found it difficult to function. She made an appointment with Dr. Daniel. He wanted to see her before he would refill her blood-pressure prescription. Dr. Daniel came from a large family and one could tell his family and friends were important to him. He was charismatic and kind. He was newly married and quickly adding new members to his family.

The nurse came in and checked her blood pressure and temperature. It was not long before Dr. Daniel came through the door. He greeted Desiree with a hug as he usually did. They spoke briefly about her health and he said everything seemed good. After he made an entry in her chart, he rolled the stool he sat on over in front of Desiree until they were eye to eye. "May I ask you something?"

"Sure."

"Has Zach ever asked you to move to Wisconsin?"

"Half heartedly, but I think if I had taken him up on the idea he would have needed medical attention."

"Well it's none of my business and don't get me wrong. Zach is good people, but I have always wondered why he can't live out in the open with the rest of us."

Desiree knew Daniel was a loyal person but she could not help believing that this conversation was a warning, and she allowed him to continue.

"Did you ever wonder why he moved up there to live in the woods? I don't get it."

"Dr. Daniel we have been together for five years and that is long enough. I am not waiting any longer."

He rolled his stool away to make another entry,

"Good for you."

He gave her a clean bill of health and a warning at the same time. It is not that easy, she thought – 'I love him.'

Two weeks later, while she was cutting a client's hair, Desiree looked up; and Zach was standing there. He had a way of appearing and disappearing that was always startling.

All he had to do was smile and she melted. Indeed, she had missed him and knew a long time ago that she was in love. They both acted as if nothing had happened and picked up right where they left off. Oddly enough, after not being home for three months, he never left her side. He took Desiree everywhere he went, as though he wanted to make sure she knew where he was at all times.

When he went back North, Desiree wondered about this odd behavior. Zach liked to be with her but he also liked to come and go as he pleased. He always wanted to visit with his friends when he came to town. The conversation with Tara came back to her, "I'll tell you what, when I come down we'll get together and discuss it, okay." 'There I go again thinking too much,' she really needed to let that silly stuff go.

Peculiar things began happening once again. At times, she would call Zach and his phone would go straight to voice mail. This had never happened before. More and more frequently, he would not answer the phone. He would sometimes call and Desiree would call him right back because she had "forgotten to tell him something." Thank God, they had unlimited calling. That was their only source to keep their long distance relationship going.

A pattern began to immerge. These odd things usually happened on a Wednesday or Friday night. The more this happened, and the dumber his excuses became, the more she tried to figure out what was going on. At what point Desiree lost touch with reality, no one is certain, she was not sure, but maybe this was it.

Zach had the same model of phone as she had and the same phone service. She did not want to accuse him of anything unless she had good reason. It seemed all Desiree had, were suspicions. She experimented with her phone to see what would make his phone go straight to voice mail.

The only things that did were when the phone was off the hook or when she was online. When she took it off the hook, it would buzz loudly for two full minutes and she knew he would not do that. He did not have the Internet as he only had an old computer Al had given him. He did not use it and, besides, he was too cheap to get it. He was always practical, and his Lowes budget did not allow for such luxuries.

She did remember recently however, she had called him and asked,

"Hey, what are you doing?"

"I am running a phone line in to my office."

"Why are you doing that?"

"In case I ever get the Internet."

It was extremely cold up there and Desiree thought it was an odd time of year to be doing that, but that was Zach. He always had to be doing something and she dismissed it. Besides, she had looked at his phone bills and there were no internet charges on the bill so she thought he could not possibly have internet.

After a while, she would deliberately call back when he called her unexpectedly. Most of the time, he would not answer, only to explain later he was out playing with Duke or he was setting traps; the list went on.

Suddenly his phone was not working. He said, with the weather up there, it could be expected from time to time. It was Wednesday night and she believed that for the first time ever he did not call all day. Even at bedtime, he did not call. Desiree was worried.

Zach called early the next morning while he was getting ready for work. He said his phone had been out the day before. When he got out of the shower and went to let Duke out, there was a tag from the phone company hanging on his door; they had been there to fix his phone.

"I thought I'd better call because I knew you would be worried." Desiree was relieved to hear from him and happy to know he was okay. Although one question he seemed to be asking more and more frequently and, as of late and it was bothering her, was,

"You're not coming up this weekend, are you?" She began to express to him that she was not comfortable with that question. What difference did it make? In addition, he would say,

"I just wanted to know."

Desiree had never met any of his co-workers nor had she ever been in Lowes. Although she wanted to, Desiree could not explain why she did not go there; he never said she could not. Desiree felt after all, that was his work place and he would be too busy to entertain her. He always told her what his schedule would be for the week and if she went up there, it was there for her to see. That soon began to change. When she would ask about his schedule, as she always had, he would say he left it at work and did not know when he was working.

"They're always changing my schedule."

Zach was always changing the rules. What was okay for her to do or ask one week was not okay the next.

Chapter 18

It was the middle of March 2004, and two weeks before he would be quitting Lowes for a position with a construction company. Desiree went up there for her usual weekend visit. The cabin, although it was always presentable, it had not been dusted since he had moved there seven months before. She was used to it. How many guys dusted their houses anyway? She was simply happy to see him.

The first thing Desiree saw when she walked through the door was the tag from the phone company from two weeks earlier. She did not say anything about it, and before the night was over, he picked it up and showed it to her. Part of Desiree was thinking 'though protests too much' while the other part, that was always trying to control her suspicious nature, accepted it and forgot about it.

That weekend, while he was the usual good host, he seemed rather standoffish. They went to bed and, because of the distance between them; their visits were usually full of passion. However, this weekend when Desiree questioned him about his lack of interest, he said,

"I am just tired."

That was the way of the entire weekend, but she guessed even men are too tired sometimes. When she left, Desiree felt empty for some reason but as Grace had always told her

"Desiree there cannot be a party going on all the time."

She went home and back to her life with Jake but she was always leaving her heart behind and wondered if their lives would ever be normal; whatever normal is. Normal to Desiree was not what her life had become, but Desiree was in love and doesn't everyone sacrifice for love?

Zach continued his daily calls and just as she was adjusting to being without him again, it would be time to go back. While Desiree was always anxious to see Zach, coming home, she was always sad to leave him.

He reassured her that, as soon as Jake went off to college, they would be together, but that was a long time off. Jake was only 12 years old. Desiree was torn. It had been almost two weeks since she had been there. On Tuesday evening when Zach called he asked, "Why don't you come up this weekend?"

"I don't know if I can, I have appointments already scheduled for Saturday. We'll see," and went on to other things. He told her he would call tomorrow.

On Wednesday, they did not discuss the weekend and he asked about her day and about Jake as he always did, and then

"Goodnight." On Thursday night, the first thing he asked was,

"You're not coming up this weekend, are you? I mean, if you are, I will call off on Friday and Saturday. If not, I will work Friday and take Saturday off. It's my last day at Lowes anyway. They have me scheduled for 11 to 8 tomorrow and Tim wants to trade his day shift, but I think I will just work 11 to 8."

"Why, it's your last day. You're a morning person and you can get it over with?"

"I'll just work 11 to 8."

That seemed odd to her but everything did these days. Desiree told him she did not think she would be coming up because she had not changed any appointments.

She went to work on Friday. Jake had gone to his dad's for the weekend and at about 5 pm, when she had finished her last client, Desiree decided to call Zach at work. She thought what can they do; fire him.

"Can I speak to Zach please?"

The operator said, "Zach's gone for the day."

"When did he leave?"

"Hold on, please." She came back,

"He left at 3 o'clock."

"Okay, thank you."

She called his house, it rang three times, and then his fax kicked in. She called a few more times a couple of minutes apart, thinking that maybe he would grab it before the third ring. He did not, so Desiree faxed him.

"Zach, call me on my cell phone as soon as you get this fax, Des." She ran home and threw a few things in her overnight bag and off to Wisconsin she went. She did not know what was going on up there, but she was going to find out. She had had it!

Desiree was driving with the music blaring, trying not to think. She had made up her mind she was going to call him every fifteen minutes until he answered. Desiree had made a silent bet with herself that if he was going to make her believe he had worked until 8 pm, he would call between 8:30 and 9:00 pm.

At 8:45 her phone rang,

"Hey, what's going on?" He seemed to be in a good mood.

"What did you work today, Zach?"

"11 to 8."

"I called work today."

"Oh yah, what did they say?"

"They said you left at 3."

"I worked an 11 to 8, but I left at 3. I went to lunch with the girl from scheduling and the guy from safety. We were drinking so I did not go back. Anyway, what are you doing?" he replied nonchalantly.

"I'm in Wisconsin."

"Get out of here, why did you do that?"

"Because I want to know what in the hell is going on up there!"

"You're crazy. You're so insecure, hurry up and get up here, where are you anyway?"

"An hour away."

"Well hurry and get your butt up here, I can't wait to see you."

Desiree pulled in to the driveway and the first thing she noticed was his truck parked in an odd place. Zach had a long driveway that circled around a tree in front of his garage. He had parked on the side of the drive and the truck was loaded with lumber. The wood was hanging about six feet off the end of his truck and there was no warning flag hanging from it. Zach was very safety conscious and this was not looking good. In fact, it was all bad.

She came in. Most times when Desiree walked through the door, he would be standing there waiting to greet her, while other times he seemed so excited to see her, he would be outside waiting. Not this time, he was lying on the couch fully dressed and looking rather nice too. She assumed he wanted to look good on his last day at work.

Desiree looked around and was stunned to see that his house was immaculately clean. There was not a dusty spot anywhere, the glass was sparkling, the bed made, and he had never done that since she met him. He always said he would be sleeping in it so why bother. The weird thing about it was the bed was made as if an Army soldier had done it, tight as a drum. It was perfect and the comforter she had bought for him was neatly folded down on his side only, as though a housekeeper had been there. Surely, she thought if this was an attempt to make it look as if he did not make his bed; he did a piss poor job. She would have jumped in it and rolled around!

Desiree felt as if she had walked into a room full of people having a party, and she was late and knew no one. She could have sworn she heard Rod Serling's voice,

"You have now entered the twilight zone."

Desiree sat down next to him on the couch and asked, "How did you go anywhere with that truck loaded with lumber?"

"We were at Applebee's and it's in the same parking lot as Lowes."

"You were at Applebee's for over five hours?"

"Well, the guy from safety wanted to go play pool and he left, so I took the girl from scheduling and her kid out for dinner."

"Where'd you go?"

"We went to Heidi's."

"You were running around with that lumber hanging out of your truck without a flag on it. That wasn't very safe and that's not like you." Without saying a word he began, running his fingers through his hair and by now, it was almost standing on end.

Desiree looked around in amazement. She could not get over how immaculate the house was so she commented,

"Boy it looks like you had company today," as she made her way to the restroom. It had been a long drive, and Desiree needed to go. She passed the long table that was against the wall next to the bathroom and noticed a dish she had bought for him. Instead of being full of the usual screws and fishing licenses, it was now full of candy. There were two different kinds, separated and very neatly placed on each side of the dish.

"Oh," she said as she walked by,

"You even have candy in your candy dish."

"It's always been there, you probably didn't notice it, because my fishing license is usually laying there."

With defiant frustration in her voice,

"Zach, that candy was not there two weeks ago." There was dead silence he was finished talking and she continued to the restroom.

Desiree tried to push all of this aside and enjoy the weekend, but she felt like Alice in Wonderland, where nothing was real and everything seemed distorted.

She did not want to be there but it was a four-hour drive, and she did not want to drive back that night. She would just make the best of it.

Zach spent the biggest part of the night trying to make sure Desiree knew nothing had gone on. Even though it all seemed so strange, he was very loving and managed to calm her down before she went to sleep.

The next morning began as it always had. Zach awakened before Desiree and as he always did, was having a cup of coffee and cooking. They enjoyed small talk over breakfast but Desiree could not seem to get comfortable. She could not put her finger on just why, but she did not feel safe.

Afterward Zach, as was his routine, got up with his coffee, and stood at the window, peering out in hopes of spotting an animal or two. Desiree made her way to another window so she could also look at nature's wonder. The trees were budding; the birds were making their way to the feeders hanging from a wire Zach had strung between two trees, not far from the fire pit. One of their favorite things to do was sit out there in the evenings. They both enjoyed those nights so much. It was a chance to relax with a drink, make conversation, or just gaze in to the flames in total silence. That was the beauty of their relationship; they felt peace even with no words spoken.

The ground surrounding the cabin was all sand and gradually became wooded. It was still wet from the night before. The wet, cold sand was like concrete until the warmth from the sun came to dry it and then it became soft and grainy once again.

Desiree noticed Duke's tracks were all around the fire pit as though he had repeatedly circled it. She then began noticing other tracks as well and they were not just dog prints, there were boot prints too. She looked down directly in front of the window. There were two sets of prints, as if set in concrete, and they were distinctly different. One was much larger than the other, and the marking on the soles were very different.

The larger one had a smooth sole, except for the heel that had many, tiny, circular markings. The smaller one had lines and arrows all over. Desiree did not know what to think, or do, so she stood there, frozen. She tried to burn those patterns in her brain. Desiree glanced over at Zach, he had moved to the window next to her. She could see him looking at her from the corner of his eye.

"What are you looking at?" he calmly asked.

"I'm just looking."

She moved away from the window and sat on the sofa, not knowing what to say or do. Zach interrupted her thoughts and asked if she would like to go for a walk.

"Yes, where are my boots?"

"They're in the laundry room."

Desiree went in the laundry room and as she was coming back in to the living room she turned her boots over to look at the soles, and again Desiree noticed Zach was looking at her from the corner of his eye. He said,

"What are you looking at, I rinsed those off?"

Wondering why he rinsed them off, she replied, "I think I will take my boots home."

"Why are you going to do that?"

"I don't want anyone else wearing my boots."

"Sweetie no one could fit in your boots."

Desiree sat down, put them on and they went for a walk. She kept looking at the prints they were leaving behind them. He was leaving little circular marks in the heel, and she was leaving lines and arrows. She did not know what to say or to accuse him of, Desiree was feeling a little like she was entering a Nancy Drew novel. She was speechless as they strolled hand in hand around his 80 acres, and Zach was making small talk.

They came back to the cabin and with enthusiasm in his voice, he said,

"Let's go in to town, and get some of the things you forgot to bring." Desiree changed in to her shoes and they went out to the truck to leave.

He said,

"Oh, that's right I dropped my keys in to the hole in the bed of the truck."

"What hole?"

"You know the one that the cap goes in to when I install it."

"How did that happen?"

"When I came home last night I laid the keys down so I could take a leak and they fell in the hole."

"Why would you go to the back of your truck on your way inside and lay them down, and then go pee?"

Now he seemed agitated,

"I don't know, but that's what I did."

Desiree looked at him in total disbelief. With no expression she could read, he looked back at her as though there was nothing strange going on. She thought, well, maybe that is possible. Surely if he were guilty, it would show on his face.

Desiree suggested if he had a good magnet, he could attach a string to it and something on his key chain must have metal in it and would grab it. Sure enough, it worked. Finally, she had had an ingenious idea. That was one of the many things she admired about Zach, he always thought outside of the box, something she always had a hard time doing. They jumped in the truck and left.

He was running all over the store pickings things up that she would need and told Desiree to go find a good book to read. When they had everything, he paid for them and they headed back to the cabin.

By the time they got back, the sun was out and all of the prints were gone. 'Too bad memories did not dissipate that easily,' she thought. Desiree had lost her chance to bring it up. She had wanted so badly to take the boots back there while he watched and show him that someone else had, indeed been wearing them. She would only look like a fool if she brought it up now.

They were only home a few minutes when the phone rang. It was Tim from work and Zach told him he would talk to him later and then he hung up. He turned to Desiree and said with a mischievous smile,

"Let's go take a nap."

Feeling exhausted but not sleepy,

"I'm going to lie on the sofa and read, you go ahead."

He called from the bedroom,

91

"Come and lay by me."

"Okay." In no time, he was snoring. The phone rang again, and Desiree asked,

"Do you want me to get that?"

"No."

As soon as it stopped ringing, he jumped up and said,

"I better get that; it might be the realtor calling about the house."

She lay there and listened as he pushed the necessary buttons to retrieve his messages and then he came back to bed.

"Who was it?"

"I don't know. The fax machine has the phone messed up." He quickly fell back to sleep and Desiree got up, went into the living room and back to the sofa, to read. She was feeling more and more uncomfortable and tried to concentrate on what she was reading, when she heard him say from the other room,

"I thought you were going to lay by me."

"I can't sleep; I will just stay in here."

The phone rang again and this time without asking, Desiree reached for the phone and answered it.

"Hello. Do you want me to wake him?"

"No, I will call back later." It was Tim again.

Finally, Zach got up, came into the living room and they spent a very quiet evening together. Tim called one more time, the conversation was short, and then the calls ended. For the first time Desiree could not wait for the next day; it could not come soon enough for her. It would be Sunday and time to go home.

She had not taken a shower or left Zach by himself for more than a minute, she did not want him making or receiving any calls. She was not going to make this any easier on him than she already had. They went to bed where Desiree tossed and turned. Finally, she got up and went back into the living room, thinking if she could just read a little, she would feel like sleeping.

She was lying on the sofa, the only sound in the room was Desiree turning the pages, and she was startled to find Zach standing at the end of the sofa, looking down at her. She felt like jumping out of her skin.

"What is wrong?"

"I can't sleep, I think I will have some ice cream, do you want some?"

"No thanks."

Zach brought his bowl of ice cream and Desiree sat up so he could sit next to her. He quietly finished, rinsed his bowl and went right back to bed. About 15 minutes later, he was standing there again. A wall was the only thing that separated them, the sofa was on one side while the bed was on the other and she did not hear him get up either time.

Without saying a word he went back to bed and the next thing she knew he was standing there, fully dressed as if he were up to stay.

"Oh, my God I did not even hear you get up much less hear you getting dressed, what is wrong?"

"I don't know I just can't sleep."

When he went to bed for the last time, Desiree wondered what he thought she was doing.

It dawned on her that all he could hear was the pages turning in her book. She looked around to see what papers he thought she might be looking at and what was in them that he did not want her to see. The only thing she saw was his spiral notebook he always had lying there. Desiree closed her book and went to bed.

The next morning, the first thing she noticed was the spiral notebook was now gone. She looked around the room and on the shelves beneath the television where he kept all of his fishing and hunting magazines. There were about 20 of them stacked up, and right in the middle was his spiral notebook.

She walked over to the window and as she was looking out, Zach came up behind her and wrapped his arms around her waist, kissing her on the back of her neck. He twirled her around, and as a little boy full of excitement would, he announced,

"Guess what, I'm coming home next weekend to see you for Easter."

Desiree smiled but did not respond, and he went on to say,

"I have to get groceries today, so I'll follow you to town and take you out for breakfast before you leave."

She still had not showered, but leaving the bathroom door open, she brushed her teeth, combed her hair, dressed, packed her bag and then they left. Desiree followed him to the Big Boy restaurant, where the server seated them in a corner booth. Zach seemed to be in a good mood, laughing and teasing her. She was happy just to be away from the cabin and maybe she was just over-thinking again.

"I do not have to be home at any certain time, so I will go with you to the grocery store." "Okay, you know Lowes has the best prices on trash bags, I will need to stop by there."

"Oh, okay," she said, believing he wanted her to go with him.

"But I still have a couple left, so I'll just wait."

With confusion in her voice,

"Why can't I meet any of your friends?"

"Sweetie, you can meet any friend I have."

Desiree relaxed, they had a nice conversation during breakfast, and she was feeling better about everything that had happened over the weekend. Zach paid the bill and she followed him to Meijer, which was near Lowes.

They laughed and chatted while he was picking through the fruit and finding the vegetables he liked, and of course comparing prices on everything. They checked out, went to his truck, and put the groceries in the back. He kissed her goodbye and said he would call her later.

He always called two or three times to make sure she was okay. He walked Desiree to her car and kissed her once again before she left. Desiree drove to the end of the parking lot and just as she was ready to pull out, she glanced in her rear view mirror. Zach was still sitting in the same parking place, smoking a cigarette.

She turned her car around, pulled up next to his truck and rolled her window down. "Something wrong?"

"No, I'm just lighting my cigarette."

She just sat there, when suddenly he sprang from the truck and said, "I think I will go back and get a price on those Adirondack chairs for the fire pit."

Okay, she thought, 'you know he is going to Lowes. You can continue to play this game, or you can go home.' She was exhausted from what felt like a cat and mouse game, so she left.

She called him while she was on the road, but did not get an answer. When she was about an hour and a half from Wilmington, She called again, he answered.

"Where were you?"

"I stopped by Dave and Suzanne's house but they were getting ready to take their Sunday afternoon nap, so I came home."

The more Desiree thought about that weekend and the further she got away from there, the angrier she became.

Chapter 19

By Tuesday, Desiree was back to work and her usual routine, but she was not over what had happened over the weekend. It seemed like when they were together, he could easily explain everything away. However, when they were apart and Desiree had time to think, she could think more clearly and realize something was wrong.

She called him from work and left a message on his voice mail.

"Zach I know you are seeing someone else and I cannot take this anymore, goodbye."

Zach had left Lowe's and was now working straight days for a contractor. That afternoon, around the time he usually got home from work, he called her at the salon, sounding very close to losing it,

"What kind of messages are you leaving on my phone? There is nothing going on up here."

"Zach, I'm with a client right now and I can't talk."

Still angry, he asked, "What time are you getting off tonight?"

"I'm working late so I'm not sure."

"If it's not too late, call me."

"Okay, goodbye."

She did not get home until 9 o'clock, 10 o'clock Wisconsin time, but she called; he did not answer. He did not call the following day, or the next and by that time, Desiree was frantic. She called several times and every time her messages got nastier, but with no response. She stopped calling and tried once again to carry on with her life and her routine.

A couple of weeks later, as they were going to Jake's soccer game, they passed Zach coming from the other direction. She did not know he was in town. He still had things to move out of his house and apparently was there to take a load back, but he never called. The following weekend there was a knock on her door and when she answered, there he was, holding a mop in his hand and a perfect smile on his face.

"I thought you might need this and I have some other things at the house that I'm getting rid of, if you can use them, you can have them."

By this time, he had worked his way into the apartment and was sitting on the sofa. Desiree sat down in the recliner, just staring at him in total disbelief. It was as if, one minute he was out of her life and like magic, he was back. She was happy to see him and did not realize, until he pointed it out, that her knees were shaking so badly, they were knocking together.

"What are you upset about?"

"I can't get over those boot prints in the sand. I want to know who was wearing my boots."

"Sweetie, there were no boot prints; I don't know what you're talking about. No one was wearing your boots."

His blue eyes were looking directly into hers and his perfect smile never left his face. Desiree thought, 'there is no way he could be lying, because if I were I would be blinking and stuttering, so he must be telling the truth.'

Within minutes, Desiree was convinced she had exaggerated the whole thing and was just feeling insecure about the distance between them. They kissed and made up. He said he was going to meet his friend, Tommy Peterson for a few drinks. She had never met Tommy. The only thing Zach had ever told her about him was that Tommy would not be where he was if it were not for him. He had said the same thing about most of his friends; they "had each other's back." They were all financially better off than he was. He certainly had sacrificed a lot for his friends. He was more concerned about their success than his own; rare loyalty she thought. Desiree told him she was also going out to meet friends at their usual place. He left and she got ready and left as well.

Desiree was there only a few minutes when Zach came walking through the door. He said that Tommy had changed his plans so he decided to come and see her. He spent the night and the weekend was great, once again as though they had never been apart. Jake was also happy to see him.

Everything went back to normal with Zach. He was calling every night and they were happy once again. Mother's Day 2004 was coming up and it was her weekend to be with Zach; Jake was going to his dad's house. She decided to go up to Wisconsin and come home early to spend time with her boys.

Jason had his family, Jett did not live in the area anymore, and Jake was with his dad, so off she went. Zach was as welcoming as ever, and had stocked the fridge with her favorite things, including chocolate. He learned a long time ago that chocolate was indeed the way to Desiree's heart; it did not take much to make her happy.

They had a routine; he would rise before Desiree and the smell of bacon would permeate throughout the cabin and wake her like an alarm clock. They would have breakfast and walk the property. Then she would help with whatever project he was working on. Zach made sure, when she went there, that they also had leisure time.

It was spring and he had finally purchased the boat he had always wanted. They were off to Hanley Lake to take it for a spin and maybe even do some fishing while they were out there. They stopped at the Meijer gas station to fill up the truck and the boat.

When they pulled up, he said,

"Oh, there's Steven from Lowes." He got out and headed to the back of the truck.

Steven yelled,

"Hey Zach, how are you?"

Zach glanced up, said hi, and kept on with whatever he was doing back there.

Steven continued to fill his tank, but Desiree could not help noticing that he was staring at her. He would then look at Zach, who seemed to be oblivious to him even being there. He would repeatedly look at him and then stare at her and was not hiding the fact that he was doing it.

Finally, he walked over to where Zach was standing, and Zach immediately said, "Sweetie can you come out here and help for a minute?"

At first, Desiree thought he was showing her off and proving to her that she indeed could be around his friends. He definitely wanted Steven to know that she was his girlfriend.

"Steven this is Desiree, Des this is Steven." They spoke for only a minute and Zach kept his back to him as though he just did not want to be bothered. Steven said goodbye and left. They got to the lake and enjoyed the rest of the afternoon. Zach had made sure they had everything they needed, food, drinks, warm clothes and shoes; he always made sure she was comfortable.

Early on Sunday morning, they had breakfast and then decided to go out and organize the garage. Zach was a pack rat and it was not an easy task but Desiree was happy just to be with him.

They spent all morning cleaning, sweeping, and moving boxes. Zach and Desiree worked well together; they always knew what each other was thinking and what the other wanted.

During their small talk, Zach mentioned four times that he wanted to rearrange his living room furniture and wanted her to help.

It was getting to be close to the time for her to go. It was Mother's Day, and she had to get back home,

"If you want me to I will help you move furniture, then I have to go." They went in and discussed how they might rearrange the furniture. They walked over to the couch and Zach said,

"It is hard telling what is under here; it hasn't been moved for eight months."

They lifted it up and surprisingly there was nothing under it, except a little dust. They moved it to another wall and then went over to the love seat that was sitting in the middle of the room; it divided the living room from the dining room.

The cover was too big for it and dragged on the floor so they removed it. They bent down at the same time and lifted it up. As they started across the room, he wanted to set it down for a minute. He looked over to the spot where it had been sitting, which made her look as well.

A long, folded envelope was lying there. The front had Zach's name on it and the front side had a Brenda's name and number in Zach's handwriting. The moment seemed to stand still; they both just stood there and finally, he bent down to pick it up.

He unfolded it and held it out bottom side up so Desiree could see that it was empty, and while she could no longer see the print on the front, she could see that it had once contained a greeting card. At first, it appeared to be a business envelope, but now she could see the logo on the back.

They both stared at it for what seemed like five minutes, but it was more like several seconds. Finally, he walked over to the wood stove and tossed it in the fire, as he did all of his paper goods, after all it saved on trash and fed the fire.

They quickly moved the love seat without saying a word and then she left. This played repeatedly in her mind the entire drive home. Everything, she thought was very strange. 'He does not acknowledge, he never has a guilty expression, and if he were guilty, it would show all over his face. Therefore, it must be me.'

The closer Desiree was to home and the further she was from Wisconsin, the more troubled she became. Zach called three or four times to make sure she had a nice Mother's Day and was getting home safely. She spent the evening with Jake and spoke to Jason and Jett when they called to wish her Happy Mother's Day.

It was Monday and there was always a lot to do. Having spent her weekend up North it only gave her one day to get groceries, clean the house, and do laundry, but that was the price she paid for dating someone long distance – and to Desiree, it was worth it.

As the day wore on the envelope kept pushing to the front of her mind. She decided to look up that phone number on the Internet. One of her clients had just told her that she had done it and it was easy. Desiree went to the website that Mariah had given her and entered the number.

The name Brenda Stiller popped up, with an address – all in less than ten seconds. The Internet is a great source of information. Although she was pretty much computer illiterate, she was learning. She went to the phone and dialed the number for Lowes.

"Can you tell me if Brenda is working today?"

"Which one?" The operator asked.

"Brenda Stiller."

"She will not be in until Saturday."

"Thank you, good-bye."

Now that Desiree knew that he worked with her and she was part time, what would she do with that information? She went back to what she needed to accomplish before Jake came home.

Later Zach called, "Hi, Sweetie, how was your day?"

"Fine, can I ask you something?"

"Sure."

"Honey, who is Brenda?"

There was a brief silence and then, in that very familiar soft soothing voice,

"A lady I worked with at Lowes," and in an even softer voice yet, he said, "Okay?"

With relief, she said,

"Okay."

He asked about Jake and wanted to know all about her day, and then he said,

"I love you, sweet dreams, and goodnight."

No matter how busy Desiree was, she just kept going back to finding the card under the love seat. There seemed to be a tug of war

.

going on in her head. She could not resolve it in her mind so she ended their relationship once again.

She began receiving strange phone calls at work, some of which came when the salon was closed. They did not leave messages. When they were separated, Desiree received strange calls from different parts of Wisconsin and even the Lowes in her area.

Just when she felt she had made the correct decision, Zach called. He asked if he could get his haircut as he was coming in for the weekend. She told him that while she would not be able to do it on Friday night; she could do it on Saturday, at noon.

Desiree planned to make it a short day so Jake and she could do something together. On Friday night, she went out with her friend, Shelly to a Mexican Restaurant. It was their girl's night out for laughs and giggles. She had to be home early so she would feel well at work the next day. She always dreaded Saturday mornings.

"Everyone should sleep in on Saturday. It should be a law, Desiree," she mumbled as she dragged herself out of bed and into the shower. Jake was watching television when she came out. She fixed his breakfast, he dressed, brushed his teeth, and then they went to work. She did not mind too much, it was going to be a short day and Desiree was sure Jake would come up with something he wanted to do.

Around twelve o'clock, Zach came through the door. He sat down in the waiting room area. He said "Hello" to Jake and then to Desiree, but he was quiet, almost in a shy way. While she was cutting his hair, they were not talking much when Jake asked,

"Mom can we go to Wal-mart, and look around when you are done?"

"Sure, I guess buddy, as soon as I am finished."

Zach asked if he could tag along, and not knowing what to say, she said okay. It was a short drive to Wal-mart and when they went in, she left him and Jake in the fishing department. Desiree wondered around looking at other things while they looked at fishing gear.

When she found them, they had their arms full of fishing lures and a brand new fishing pole for Jake, heading to the checkout counter. Jake's eyes seemed to light up when Zach was around. He was happy to see him; after all, he usually spent most of his time with Desiree.

They left, heading home and on the way back, Zach suggested,

"Why don't we go to the store and get some steaks to cook on the grill. I'll take Jake fishing at the pond after we eat?"

"That's up to you guys." He headed to Stop and Shop.

Zach and Jake were busy talking while Desiree was going along for the ride. Zach grilled steaks and they sat together as a family to have dinner. She left the dishes in the sink and they took off for the pond to fish.

Desiree stayed for a few minutes and told them she would let them hang out together while she went back to clean up. They did not have much luck and after about an hour, they came home.

Desiree was still cleaning up when they came in, laughing and talking. Zach came in to the kitchen and announced,

"I am just going to stay here tonight, if you don't mind."

"I don't mind if you stay, Zach, but you will have to sleep on the sofa."

He turned and headed back in to the living room, picking up his things along the way, and set them on the table as if he was about to leave. He then sat down on the sofa. The thought ran through her mind, that if she did not know better she would consider his behavior a threat. They were all sitting there watching sports, when he turned to her and said,

"I am supposed to be in Wisconsin right now. I promised the boys I would take them out on the boat today." Desiree did not respond, and within a few minutes, he got up, and said that he was going to leave.

He walked over to Jake and gave him a hug, and told him, he had to go, and to take care. As he was almost to the door, he turned and asked if Desiree would walk him to his truck. She followed behind him and when they got to the parking lot, he pulled out his wallet. He took out a piece of paper, and handed it to her.

"What is this?"

"I paid your car off; I know you are trying to buy that town home, and I thought that it might help." She had six more payments left on her car.

"How did you know where I had this loan, and how did they let you do this?"

"It wasn't easy," he replied.

She looked up at him; tears began streaming down his face. She had never seen Zach cry in the four years they were together.

"What is wrong?"

"I know that you are what I want, and I want to spend the rest of my life with you, but I am so scared."

"What are you afraid of?"

"I am afraid that I won't be able to go fishing and hunting." Tears were dripping from his chin.

Desiree walked over to Zach and with her hands; she gently wiped his face. "Zach, you know I would never keep you from doing what you love to do. I would not want you to keep me from doing things with my kids."

"I would never keep you from your kids." Then suddenly he said,

"I have to go."

"What?"

"I have to go, I need to think."

"After everything you just said, you are leaving?"

"I'm going back to Wisconsin, I need to think." He got in his truck, and he was gone. Desiree was reeling from what had just happened and went back to her apartment, shaking her head. She did not hear from him for two weeks.

She decided to go down to Lakeside, a little bar in town. Her friends were always there on Friday night. She did not go out much and needed a break. The bar was hopping and while Desiree enjoyed herself, she did not stay long. Jake was at home, and she did not want to leave him home alone.

Zach had called while Desiree was out so she returned the call, after Jake went to bed. "What are you doing?"

"I am putting in a hot water heater. I was thinking about you, so I thought I would call."

He mentioned that FBI agents had stopped by. " What did they want?"

"They were looking for someone," and he changed the subject.

"I want to invite you to come up here for the 4th of July, for the fireworks. You do not have to give me an answer right now, think about it, and let me know. I will call you tomorrow, goodnight, and sweet dreams."

He called, the following afternoon, wondering if Desiree had decided whether she was coming or not. She had thought about it, and decided he must have made his decision. He would probably propose, on the boat, under the stars, while watching the fireworks; what could be more romantic than that.

Desiree went to visit friends and told them what had happened. Ken looked at her and said,

"Don't go."

"What?"

"He is not going to ask you to marry him; he wants to see if he can get it back the way that it was." She respected Ken, he had always given good advice, but this time, he was wrong, she was sure of it.

Jake went to his dad's and Desiree packed her bags and went to Wisconsin. When she got there, it was as if they had never parted. Even when they did nothing, it was great just being together. This time was even going to be better, she was certain of that.

They got all of their necessary gear together and Zach had packed their cooler to the brim. They set off for the lake, and as they always did, stopped by to see Benny and Mae.

They were friends of Zach's that he had known for years. They had a cottage on the lake and always welcomed her with open arms.

Zach suggested they go out with them on their pontoon. Desiree was a little disappointed, but the night was young, who knows?

It was an enjoyable evening, catching up on the latest gossip and listening to Benny's latest jokes. Zach and Desiree went to the back of the pontoon, and lay down; he wrapped a blanket around her and held her, while a beautiful explosion of color lit up the sky. After many 'oohs and ahhs,' they went back to the cottage, built a fire, talked, and laughed until late that night. By this time, Desiree realized, Ken was right.

She made the best of the next day until it was time to go home. She was disappointed, but Desiree knew she loved him. If he was not quite ready, she knew that he loved her, and it would happen – eventually.

They resumed their relationship and Desiree was happy to do so, even though she got the old "I told you so" from Ken when she got home. A couple more weeks went by and Desiree decided to ask him, why he did what he did.

He explained to her that if they got married, he would not be able to claim homestead on his cabin. She was furious,

"You mean you are choosing money over me!"

"No, sweetie, but you need to use your head, think about it, there are many reasons why it is not a good idea, right now. You need to do what you do, let me do what I do, and when Jake turns 18, and then we can be together. We both have a lot going on right now, and it is not a smart thing to do."

Desiree was upset, but when she thought about it; he was right. She could not go up there, until Jake went away to school and she certainly could not take him there, away from his school, his friends, and their family. Jake was only 12, so she had a long wait, but who knows, maybe Zach would change his mind, move back home, and do it sooner.

Why Desiree kept going back was a continuing mystery to her. She always felt confused, but when Zach explained things to her, everything he said made sense.

Once again, he began telling her she was too suspicious, too jealous, and she just needed to calm down. She did not need to know everything. When Desiree asked if he always told her everything, as she did him, he replied,

"I tell everything you need to know."

Desiree had been acting a little crazy in the past, and maybe she was a little crazy, but she knew one thing, she was madly in love with him. She pushed all of her feelings aside, while feeling sometimes, that somehow, she was absorbing his.

Chapter 20

Zach received some bad news. Mr. Bevan, Sheila's father, whom he had been very close to, had passed away. Apparently, he had suffered from cancer for a while. He called Desiree to let her know he would be coming in to town. "Al called me and said Sheila said I was not welcome to come to the wake."

"That's awful," Desiree responded in total disbelief, "you were close to him, I don't understand that at all."

"Well, I am coming to pay my respects. I'm going to stay an extra few days so I can help you move too." She was happier that he would be staying longer than she was that he would be helping her move.

The night of the wake, Desiree went with him to get a tie for the suit he would be wearing. In his blue suit and gold tie, he looked as though he had walked out of GQ magazine when he left.

He was gone for several hours and Desiree was beginning to worry when he walked through the door.

"Boy I am so glad that I am with you." He wrapped his arms around Desiree and kissed her.

"What happened?"

"Al met me at the door and told me to make it short and sweet. Apparently, Sheila did not want me there. They put her in a separate room while I was there."

"If they said make it short and sweet, why were you gone so long?"

"I ended up staying for over two hours."

"Why did you do that? Did she stay in another room the entire time you were there?"

"Yes, I couldn't help it. Everyone came up and wanted to talk to me. Benny and I went for a drink afterwards."

Desiree could not help but feel sorry for Sheila. Here she was, afraid of Zach for some reason and she could not be in the same room with him at her own father's wake.

By August, her feelings came bubbling back to the surface. Zach called one Sunday afternoon,

"I came home last night, and there were tire tracks in my driveway. I went around the cabin a couple of times before I went in." Desiree thought that was a little extreme just because there were tire tracks in the driveway. 'I guess he is being cautious,' she thought.

He said he was outside, it was a beautiful day, and he was having a cocktail, playing with Duke. He was in an unusually good mood, and getting ready to grill a couple of chicken breasts. He was going to eat and play with Duke for a while.

When he said a couple of chicken breasts, she wondered. 'There I go again, thinking the worst, so what if he was an in an exceptionally good mood, and so what, if she had never seen him eat more than one chicken breast at a meal before.'

He said,

"I'll call you later."

About a half an hour later, she tried calling him; he did not answer the phone. Desiree waited a little while, and tried again, no answer. Four hours later, he answered, nonchalantly as though they had just spoken, and by this time, Desiree had worked herself into a frenzy.

"Where have you been?"

"Right here, why?"

"I have been calling you for the past four hours."

"I was out, playing with the dog."

"Your phone was outside, when you called earlier, why didn't you answer it?"

"Sweetie, you should not get so upset. Maybe you need to go talk to someone, and get medication. Calm down."

She hung up the phone,

"That's it, I am done." She jumped in the shower, got dressed, and went out and met her friends.

When she got there, Abby told her that, a friend of a friend wanted to meet her, but she had told him, he was on his own. He finally made his way up to introduce himself and while she thought he was cute, he was short and not her type. He had a great smile and a great line as well. He began calling, came over a few times, and he brought dinner to her house; he was a great cook. She went over to his house. He had invited Desiree to dinner, but while he seemed nice, he also seemed more than ready to get physical, and she certainly was not ready for that. Zach and Desiree had only been apart for a few weeks, and as he was moving excessively fast, she ended it.

Unexpectedly, Zach called, and once again, they were back together. However, it was not long before strange things began happening again. His phone was going straight to voicemail or he was not answering it.

Desiree arranged for all of her kids and grandkids to go with her to see her mother. She was feeling uneasy as it was nearing the three-year mark and Katy said she kept talking about Jason for some reason. She obviously had shown love for all of her boys but had brought him up several times. When they got there, she seemed okay at first, but within an hour, Grace asked if she could go back to bed, and that was not her mom. Jason followed her to her room and sat on the floor next to her bed where they talked.

Desiree busied herself making the fudge Grace had so patiently taught her to make as a young girl. She poured it in the plate and while waiting for it to harden, divvied out the rest with spoons to whoever wanted some; a family tradition they followed from their childhood days on 45th Street.

She cut the fudge into squares and took two pieces to take to Grace. Desiree knew she loved to eat it while it was still warm. The lights were dim and Desiree quietly made her way into her room; Jason kissed her on the forehead and joined the rest of the family in the living room. Grace looked up and smiled as Desi sat on the edge of the bed next to her. "Honey," she said in a somewhat weaker voice,

"Could you set this on the nightstand, I will eat it later?" Seeing the disappointment and fear in Desiree's eyes, while hers were lighting up, she said,

"I am spoiled rotten."

Knowing better than that and holding back her tears Desiree retorted,

"Mom, you have never had a spoiled rotten day in your life."

Still showing a gleam in her eyes, she responded,

"Oh yes I have."

"When were you ever spoiled?"

Desiree could see her mother's mind taking her back and she smiled,

"My dad use to spoil me rotten."

Remembering some of the stories she had heard, Desiree asked,

"How did he spoil you?"

Possibly the saddest thing Grace had ever said to her as she simply replied,

"He made me breakfast."

She paused for a moment and continued in her weak and broken voice, but still with a smile on her face and a light in her eyes, she replied as a little girl would,

"Sometimes I ate it and sometimes I didn't."

She did not know how she managed to hold herself together. That is what a parent is supposed to do. The fact that this stood out in her mind after over 70 years, spoke volumes. Her voice broke up Desiree's thoughts once again,

"If I make it till spring I want to go back to Elcho."

"Mom, I took you there not long ago. Do you think it is ever going to look again as it did when you were young?"

Her eyes and her smile seemed bigger and brighter, when she calmly said,

"I just want to go back down that road."

Desiree would never see Grace alive again.

It was November 2004, hunting season, when friends came up to join Zach for the opener of shotgun season. Benny was there, asleep on the sofa, while Al was due in anytime. Zach always looked forward to this week, spending time with his friends, and having a few drinks. He was a great host, very accommodating, always making sure that everyone felt at home.

He called Desiree on that day to let her know he was waiting for Al, and that he was thinking of her, and would talk to her later. Desiree always knew that during these times, Zach would only be calling at bedtime, so she did not expect more than that.

She remembered something that she forgot to tell him, so she called him right back. "Hello."

"Hey."

"Hey, what's going on?"

"What do you mean; I just spoke to you a minute ago, I'm at work?"

"Oh," he said, "I didn't know it was you."

"You hear a woman's voice, and you say, 'Hey, what's going on?' Who did you think you were speaking to?"

Without a pause he answered,

"Sweetie, there's a lot going on, the dog was barking, and Dave was coming through the door, I apologize." They spoke briefly and then they said goodbye. For the next three days he apologized repeatedly, which made Desiree more uncomfortable.

The following week, Jake and Desiree were going there to spend Thanksgiving with Zach. She thought he could not possibly be seeing anyone else, because she spent every holiday with him, so she let it go.

However, after a few days and having that gut feeling that would not go away, she ended the relationship. Every time was going to be the last but Desiree, so far could never seem to make it stick. She called and left a message, telling him she would not be coming for Thanksgiving.

It probably was not the correct way to handle it, but she knew if they spoke, he would say she was crazy, and she did not want to go through this anymore.

She did not hear from him until early December, when she received a letter telling her how much he cared. He knew that she felt she needed more from him and for that, he was sorry, but he could not give it to Desiree.

He wished her mother well; she was now in the latter stages of her cancer and was not going to be with them for much longer. She called him, and after talking, they decided they had been together too long not to continue with their relationship.

He was laid off from his job; he had been working for a construction company. He asked,

"What are you doing for Christmas?"

"Aren't you coming down? You always spend Christmas with us."

"Sweetie, I already have plans."

"What plans?"

"Well, Mom and Trish are coming up here for Christmas; these arrangements were made while we were apart."

"Okay, I understand. I'll come up the weekend before so we can celebrate together."

Desiree went up there as promised, bringing him Poinsettias as she always did. He was always bringing Desiree flowers and it was the least she could do. She brought gifts along and he said that he had some for her as well.

They had a wonderful time together, candle-lit dinners and snuggling in bed, while watching television. On Saturday afternoon while Desiree was preparing dinner, Zach wanted to go hunting. He bundled up, grabbed his gun, and off he went.

The phone rang and when she answered it, his mom asked, "Hi Desiree is Zach around?"

"He is out back, hunting."

"Oh, are you staying up there for Christmas?"

"No, aren't you and Trish coming here?"

"No, we're going to Katy's house for a visit." Katy was Zach's older sister.

Feeling somewhat confused, "Oh, okay."

"Please ask Zach to call me, when he comes in."

"I sure will, Merry Christmas."

"You too, bye."

She sat down on the sofa, thinking about their phone conversation. She could have sworn Zach said his mother was coming and that was why he would not be able to come down.

As Desiree pondered this, she noticed that on the coffee table, peeking from beneath some mail, some Christmas cards lay open. He had some displayed and she wondered why these were not. Maybe he just had not had time to do it. She picked up the first one and it was from his old roommate, who had moved to Kentucky. The second one was from Matthew and Lisa. Lisa had written a little note inside. 'Zach, we are looking forward to seeing you on the 22nd or maybe sooner' Love, Matthew and Lisa.

Zach came walking through the door. She told him his mother had called, and she wanted him to call her back.

"I thought you said your mom was coming here for Christmas. She told me she and Trish are going to Katy's, and why does this Christmas card from Matthew and Lisa say that you're coming down on the 22nd?"

Without skipping a beat,

"I was going to surprise you, but mom blew it, just wait until I call her." He strolled over to the phone and returned his mother's call. Laughter in his voice, he said,

"Thanks for blowing my surprise, Mom. Desiree didn't know I was coming down."

The night before she was leaving to go home, Zach surprised her,

"Guess what, I'm going home with you. I'll follow you back to Indiana." She was so excited; they would be spending some much-needed time together. This was better than any Christmas present he could have given her.

His friends had planned a get together on the 23rd at a nearby restaurant, and she was invited. Lisa and Matthew arrived a little late, and when Lisa gave Zach a hug, looking over his shoulder she was evidently surprised to see Desiree. Desiree overheard her ask,

"Is that, Desi, Zach?"

She came over and said hello, and everyone began talking, ordering drinks, and celebrating.

She was not feeling comfortable and about that time, Desiree heard a man yell across the room, "There's my hairdresser." It was her ex-fiancé Dane, who was having a party of his own.

Everyone at his table was laughing, and seemed to be genuinely having a good time. Desiree kept thinking 'I wish I were over there;' she just did not fit in.

When they left, Zach commenting more than asking,

"What was up with you tonight, you were not acting right?"

"I was fine."

Chapter 21

Christmas morning, 2004 was another good one, with everyone together. There was Christmas music in the background and wrapping paper knee deep. All the hustle and bustle early in the day followed by a quiet evening on the sofa; it was the best.

One evening just after the holiday Zach suggested, "Let me take you out for dinner."

"Okay, let's go to Applebee's, we can use your gift card that Jeff sent you."

"I don't have it with me."

"Where is it?" she asked.

"I cleaned out my wallet and left it at home."

"Okay, I guess we can go there, anyway."

They talked about her mom. Desiree began reminiscing "Remember the day I told Jake about Grandma telling her to only pick up pennies that were heads up, and that they are good luck?" He smiled.

They had pulled up to her apartment in Zach's truck. When Jake opened the door, he yelped with delight, "Look Mom – pennies, and they are heads up." She did not see him bend down to pick them up and just as Desiree was slamming the door – he stood up. His head was caught between the truck and the door. He was no longer yelping with delight; he was yelping in pain– so much for good luck.

Grace was losing her battle, and Desiree could not get over how courageous she had been. Her determination and will to live had kept her with them. However, the aggressive stage of the cancer she was in was about to surpass Graces' will to survive.

Desiree told Zach she was going to have to go there soon, as she wanted to spend some time with her. He agreed that it was probably a good idea.

Zach decided to stay through New Year's so they could celebrate together and that was one of their special holidays to be together, so Desiree was happy. They did not go out on New Year's Eve; they preferred to spend a quiet evening at home.

It was unusually warm for this time of year. Living in the Midwest, one could expect extreme conditions. It was very cold in the winter and very hot in the summer. Everyone looked forward to spring and fall, but those seasons were short.

Earlier that day they took Duke to the park to get some exercise, and to wear him out; he had a lot of energy. Desiree decided she should call her mom, as she always did at least once a day.

"Hi Mom, how are you?" Surprisingly she sounded good.

Recently, she had been acting strange. She did not want to talk, and she thought Katy and Brianna were trying to kill her. She did not act as if she knew to whom she was speaking. In her broken speech, because of her stroke, she managed to get out,

"I am okay."

"Do you know who this is?"

"Yes, it is Desiree."

"Sing me a song Mom."

She began to sing, "Hallelujah, Hallelujah."

"I love you, Mom."

"I love you to, honey, bye, bye." That would be the last conversation Desiree would ever have with her mother.

She had planned to go the following weekend to visit until she got a call from Braden. He had left the rehab center so he could be with Grace.

"I'm going to tell you what Katy told me. I mentioned to her, you were planning a visit for next weekend and she said if you want to visit with Mom, you should come before then."

Not knowing what to do, Desiree called Katy. Katy said she was afraid to say for sure but she thought that Mom's life was nearing the end.

Her kidneys were shutting down and there were other signs as well. Desiree told her she would make arrangements and she would be there sooner. She turned to Zach and relayed what Katy had told her. He said he thought that maybe she should consider going right away.

Desiree called Brianna to update her. Brianna said she would begin packing and would be ready whenever she was. Another call came in and Desiree was not sure who took the call, or even who had called, but they needed to leave right away.

Zach left to go back to Wisconsin, He explained he had to go back to pay his taxes. He left $100 on the counter. Desiree drove the 45 miles to Rob and Brianna's house, and Rob drove them to Tennessee. It was a painfully quiet trip, unlike the ones in the past, which were full of anticipation and excitement.

Desiree asked that no one call her while they were on the road. She did not feel she could handle that kind of news so far away. It was late when they reached the mountain and the long winding road seemed endless. The night was still and the house was dark but for one single light in the living room. Desiree saw silver hair glistening in Grace's recliner. She exhaled.

Brianna and Desiree walked in together and her elation turned to despair when she realized the silver hair belonged to her sister. Desiree looked around the room, only to see the empty hospital bed where Grace had laid.

Grace's pajamas that she had sent her for Christmas were neatly folded on the bed, along with the warm, fuzzy slippers she had given her, and the blanket that Brianna had given her.

Brianna, Katy, and Desiree held each other and sobbed. They cried for Grace and they cried for themselves.

Desiree did not get to hold her hand, kiss her, or say good-bye; it was Monday January 3, 2005.

Their visits were over. No more laughing or crying together, no more fussing at her, no more planting rose bushes for her on Mother's Day, no more giving her showers, no more dreaded cleaning up after the woman who had always cleaned up after her – no more.

Desiree went outside and called Zach to give him the news and to find out when he would be coming.

"Sweetie I am so sorry, but the weather's bad and it's too far to drive, I won't be coming." Desiree knew that she did not hear what she thought she heard. She began to plead.

"This is my mom we're talking about" she cried,

"I will never have another mom."

"I know sweetie. I am sorry."

"Zach, you have to come."

"Listen Sweetie, do you want me to die too? There is a snowstorm and you want me to drive 900 miles. There is nothing I can do." She was too distraught to argue; maybe he did have a point.

Desiree hung up the phone and went to Grace's house, went to her room, crawled in her bed and she wept. She stayed in her bed all of the following day; it was comforting to her. The scent of Grace was there. She lay there and looked all around her room; Desiree wanted to see what her mother had seen every day for a very long time.

Every one grieves differently, but for Desiree, she wanted to be as close to her mom as she could be; that was the only way she knew how to do it. She bathed in her shower, used her toiletries, and wore her slippers.

Timothy was there with their sons; Jake decided he wanted to remember his Grandma the way she was. He could not get over how his Uncle Reagan had looked in his casket. He had asked,

"Mom, why does he look like that?" He decided to stay with his best friend, Tad.

Desiree had let go of all of the abuse that her ex had delivered and, while the scars remained, this was not the time for her to bring up their past. He asked if she needed a ride home after the funeral. Brianna had decided to stay a little longer, but Desiree needed to get home to Jake and back to work, so she accepted.

It was difficult to leave her mom behind. Desiree had wanted her back in Indiana, the place she had called home for so many years. Katy made the decision to keep her close to her. She had taken care of Grace for a long time and Desiree felt it was not the time to argue about this, after all, she was not in that grave; she would remain with her always.

Later that evening Timothy stopped at a gas station and Desiree took the opportunity to call Zach. She wanted to let him know that she was on her way home. When he answered, he said that he was on the phone talking to Al and asked if he could call her back. She was furious and responded,

"Tell him you will call him back."

In an irritated voice, he said, "Hold on."

He returned to her and said, "What is your problem?"

"My mother just passed away, her funeral was today, I am on the road, and you wanted to continue to make small talk with Al?" He was very short with her, and maybe due to the circumstances she was overreacting so Desiree said goodbye.

When she finally got home, she went straight to bed. Zach's friend, Tim from Lowes called and seemed surprised to hear her voice,

"I am sorry to hear about your mom." I will let you go, take care." Zach said later that Tim was calling another Desiree programmed in his cell phone; he had not meant to call her.

Later Zach called,

"You are lucky I did not tell you to f--- off and that I didn't hang up on you last night." This was the worst time in her life, why was he being so cruel but once again, this was not the time to start something, – and after all, Desiree was overly sensitive these days.

She was always questioning her judgment and her behavior but she was always the one in turmoil and in an emotionally bad place; he seemed to rise above emotions and to her that displayed strength.

She felt she should listen to someone who was in a better place. More and more though, she was questioning him. While she could not put her finger on what was going on, something did not feel right to her. There were times Desiree felt he was lying. She would question him, only to find out he was telling the truth, and then she questioned herself.

Desiree could not help feeling bitterness when Zach did not come to pay his respects to her mom. He did not send flowers, and her family and friends were outraged.

She had lost her sister, Diana, her brother and now, her mother; Desiree did not know how much more she could take. A break up would be too much.

Zach began coming to Indiana more often, getting small remodeling jobs. He had been on unemployment and was having a difficult time getting work. Up to that point, he had refused to work for any of her clients. "Mixing business with a relationship does not work, I know from experience," he would say. He would stay with Jake and Desiree whenever he came. They both loved his visits; their house seemed more like a home. It always erased whatever doubts she had.

Jake had always wanted to be a part of a family, and he felt safe when Zach was there. He did not double check the locks anymore and, with Duke there, that even made it better; he slept like a rock and seemed to be in a better mood during those times. He had grown to love Zach.

Her good friend Shelly and Desiree had planned a trip to Las Vegas. Zach was happy to take care of Jake while she was away. It would just be the boys hanging out.

It was early April and finally after many attempts of trying to get Zach to do jobs for her clients, he agreed to do one.

Las Vegas was always fun, where night turning in to day and back to night means nothing. After four days, however Desi was more than ready to come home. Zach had been calling as early as 6:30 am, which seemed a little odd. Shelly laughed and said, "That boy is a freak."

When she walked into the house, there was a roaring fire in the fireplace, flowers and Zach was setting the table, complete with candles. He had prepared dinner, barbecued ribs. After dinner as he had done so many times, he removed her shoes and as ordered, she lay on the sofa for a foot massage. It was a wonderful welcome home.

The next evening she went up in to her office and jumped on the computer. There was an icon on her desktop, she had never seen. It was a picture of a blonde woman with the word 'sex' captioned under it. Just then, Jake walked in the room and said, "I saw that too Mom, I don't know where it came from."

Desi tried to delete the file and every time, it would pop back up. The computer was freezing up and moving slow. She thought someone had probably hacked in and now it was crashing.

When Zach finished with Saundra's basement, Desiree told him another client wanted him to build a deck for her. While he did not seem too enthused, he reluctantly said he would stop by and look at it. He decided, after meeting her, he would build it, and he planned to start soon.

It had been a few weeks since her Vegas trip, and she was back to her routine. Desiree grabbed the mail on her way in from work and threw it on the table, making a mental note to look at it later. She needed to get dinner started, and over so she could relax before going to bed.

Chapter 22

After dinner the next evening, while sitting at the table, Zach and Desiree were talking about how their day had gone when she reached over and picked up the phone bill. She casually opened it while they were chatting. The amount shocked her.

She rarely looked at the details of the bill; she just wrote the check and mailed it. However, this time she decided to dissect it to see if there was a mistake. She noticed some unusual calls that were very expensive. She told Zach she would call the phone company the next day to see what these charges were, and they continued their conversation.

The next day she looked at the charges again. Desiree noticed the calls were around 11:30 at night during the time she was in Las Vegas. She dialed the number on the bill and explained to the woman that she had been incorrectly charged for those calls.

Zach was sitting there, reading the paper oblivious to the conversation. The woman assured her that someone at her house had made these charges, via the Internet. It was an adult pornographic site. Desiree was furious, "No one in this house was on this site. My son goes to bed between 9 and 9:30 at night. There is no way he is up at that time of night."

"Ma'am, I will remove these charges this time but I suggest that since you have dial up, you call the phone company and put a block on your phone. I also want you to know that someone inside that house was on that site; no one hacked in to your computer. It does not work that way."

Ignoring the operator's last comment, Desiree was determined that if someone had hacked in, it would not happen again.

"While I have you on the phone, there are some calls I did not make on this bill."

"Ma'am, these are two calls to Las Vegas information, but I will take them off of your bill as well."

She turned to Zach and said,

"She told me, these were two calls to information in Las Vegas. How weird is that, those calls were made the day after I came home." Desiree immediately called to put a block on her phone.

Was she overreacting? No one seemed to think this was a big deal. She thought that this was the strangest thing and that it was even stranger that she was the only one making a big deal of it.

The computer was useless, pages kept popping up, and it seemed to take on a life of its own. After hours of trying to get it to stop, she decided to take it to the Geek Squad and have them look at it. Desiree went downstairs, laughing and told Zach the computer was possessed, and she thought this would probably be a good subject for a movie. As funny as she felt that scenario was, strangely enough; he did not respond.

The next day, her phone had no dial tone; Desiree said aloud,

"Boy if it were not for bad luck I wouldn't have any at all." She went to her cell phone and called the phone company. They put her on hold while they checked her line. When she came back, she told her the problem was inside her house, and there would be a charge to have them come out. Desiree told her to send someone out today if possible. The woman said she would send someone in the early afternoon.

She called Zach,

"You are not going to believe this, but my phone is not working, someone is coming to look at this afternoon." She did not have time to talk; she had to get to work, so she told him she loved him and she would come home around the time the phone company came.

Desiree got home just in time and the man asked,

"Where's your gray box?"

"I don't know."

They looked in the laundry room and then went outside. He located it on the side of the building. He said,

"Usually there is one box per home, but since this is an old building, all four units are in one box. They don't do that anymore"

He went on to explain,

"Each box now holds only the number that is inside the building it's attached to."

About that time, Zach pulled in to the driveway and got out. She walked over to his truck, and he said,

"Just go on back to work; I will stay here until this guy leaves."

As he kissed her goodbye, she proudly stated,

"You are always here when I need you, thanks."

She jumped in her car, backed around his truck and went back to work, knowing he would take care of it. When she got home, Zach and Jake were there. They were preparing dinner so she would not have to.

"Oh, by the way, (as he was handing her the bill from the phone company) he did not charge you."

"What was wrong?"

"I don't know, he didn't say."

"That's funny, how did you do that? You could sell ice to an Eskimo."

Within a few days, Zach seemed restless and distant but he assured her nothing was wrong.

The following day Desiree mentioned,

"By the way Darlene called, she has a question." She had finally convinced Zach to take a job, building a deck for Darlene.

"Why don't you just give her my phone number, so she can just call me directly?"

That hurt her feelings; it was not so much what he said but the way that he said it. The next day, Zach told her Darlene would not be home and she should stop by and visit with him while he was finishing the deck.

She had now decided that she wanted him to remodel her basement as well. Darlene seemed to be gradually becoming dependant on him. Desiree was sunning in her lounge chair when she walked up.

"Oh, you decided to check up on him." Desiree laughed, but Darlene said nothing; surely, she was teasing.

The following week Zach asked if she wanted to come with him to Darlene's house. He was going to get everything off the floor in the basement so when they came back from Wisconsin, he could get started. She began moving things off the carpet so he could remove it and as always, they worked very well together.

Desiree instinctively knew what he needed her to do. Darlene came home, and when she came downstairs, she seemed surprised to see her there again, but she did not mention it this time.

They were finished in no time and standing at the back door. Darlene handed Zach some money as they were leaving, and Desi was the first one out the door. When she turned around to say something to Zach, he had closed the door behind her. She reached over and opened it, thinking it closed accidentally but when she did, he closed it again, saying,

"You are pretty nosy."

She went to the truck and waited for him. He came out in a couple of minutes and they did not speak on the way home. It was a quiet evening and that was okay as they were going to Wisconsin the next day and would have plenty of time to talk then.

He did not seem excited about going, which was unusual for him. Normally he would be in a great mood, knowing that they were getting away, but lately he seemed to be a million miles away.

Desiree went to work the following morning; it was only a half day as they were leaving about 1:00 pm. She had lost her desire to go too – She did not know why. She just had a strange gut feeling.

Desiree came through the door expecting to see Zach running around, doing last minute things, only to find him lying on the couch.

"Are you ready to go?"

"I guess." He lay there a little longer and finally got up, went outside to pack the truck so they could leave. Duke jumped up in the truck; he seemed to be the only one that wanted to make this trip.

As usual, Zach was looking for deer on the side of the highway as he drove, while her thoughts drifted back to a conversation she had with one of her clients after they had gone to Wisconsin two weeks prior. He worked for the phone company.

She asked him about the gray box.

"Kent, if there is more than one phone number in a gray box, what does that mean?" Sometimes she asked questions or made comments that she was surprised at and had no idea where they came from.

They had gone to Wisconsin right after the phone company had come to fix the phone. Zach and Desiree had gone outside to take a walk and when they passed his gray box, she asked him if she could look inside and he said, sure.

She was curious to see what the technician was talking about when he was at her house. She opened it,

"There is your phone number, but whose number is this?"

"Remember, I told you I ran a second line in case I ever get the Internet."

"And they gave it a number?"

He seemed perplexed and said,

"I guess." She did not bring it up again but it kept nagging at her.

She asked Kent

"If there are two numbers in the box that means there are two numbers in that house."

"If you run a second line in the house but were not using it, would they give that line a number?"

He laughed,

"No Desi, if they give it a number, then it's a working line and that person is being charged to use that number. I don't know what he's up to but you can bet it's no good whatever it is, be careful."

Zach stopped by a store to pick up a part he needed while Desiree waited in the truck. They were about an hour away from the cabin when a loud noise came from under the truck. The truck was jerking and it felt as if something was about to fall out. He was not in a good mood and now it was worse. He said he thought the transmission was going out.

They made it there and he did not seem concerned about the transmission any longer. They went in and he was looking at the part he had purchased, when Desiree relayed to him what Kent had told her.

He looked up at her and said,

"I don't give a shit what he said, I only have one phone number, do you want to look at my phone bill?"

"No Zach, I don't."

He went in to the restroom. Desiree went over to the phone and dialed the number, and to her surprise, it was a working number. It went to an automated voicemail so she left a message, feeling foolish as she called three times.

When he came out, she told him what she had done. He was now more furious than she had ever seen him, and with all of the other things she had accused him of lately, he seemed to be overreacting this time. He headed for the door that leads to the garage, turned and in a threatening tone said,

"We are about done; you need to stay out of my business." The more he warned her to stay out of his business, the more she pried into it.

A few minutes later, the phone rang. She went over to get it, so she could take it to him. When she looked at caller id she realized, it was the number she had called. Desiree went to the garage wondering why Zach did not come in and answer his phone. He was standing next to the door, and so was the phone.

"Zach, I owe you an apology, the person that has that number just called."

In a cocky voice and not looking up, he asked,

"Did you answer it?"

"No."

"Why not?"

"I am sorry." She turned and went back in the cabin. Desiree picked up the phone and dialed the number.

"I am sorry for calling you, I dialed the wrong number." An angry male voice shot back, "Three times?"

"Yes, I apologize." With that, he hung up.

Zach came in and said he was going to start a fire and if she wanted, she could come out back. Desiree sat on the big log swing he had bought for her, while he pulled a chair up on the opposite side of the fire.

She asked if he wanted a beer, he said sure, so she went in, brought one out, and handed it to him. He thanked her and that was the extent of their conversation that night. His sister, Trish called. He got up and went around to the front of the property to speak to her.

Desiree got up and decided to go for a long walk around the property; Duke jumped up and followed her. Duke did not leave her side the entire time she was there. Even when Zach called him, he would not leave her. She was certain he sensed his master's anger and her sadness.

When she came back, he told her he was going in to take a shower and she went in too. He came out fully dressed, in a long sleeved shirt and sweat pants – it was summer.

He may as well have put a suit of armor on and held up a neon sign saying, 'leave me alone.' The most Zach wore when he came from the shower was shorts and most of the time those came off when he came to bed. However, not this night, he slept in his sweats.

The next morning Zach was busy in the garage and other than good morning, he did not have much to say. There was no bacon sizzling, no "Good morning baby," – nothing. He told Desiree he would be taking her home on Sunday morning rather than Monday as they had planned.

He needed to go back North right away, because he needed to have the transmission fixed on his truck. He was going to borrow his friend Dave's car to take her home. Desiree was trying to think of someone who could come and get her. She was feeling uncomfortable and unwelcome, but it was a four-hour drive up there so she decided to wait it out.

He left her in the cabin most of the day so she took a mid-morning nap. She tried to make herself at home so she went outside and started the grill. She went back in and prepared hamburgers and vegetables for lunch.

When it was finished, she could not find Zach anywhere and set out in the back to get him. She could hear his tractor and headed in that direction. She finally spotted him; he was clearing the paths that went around the property.

He glanced up and Desiree tried to motion for him to come and eat but he looked away and continued. She followed him and when she saw that he did not intend to acknowledge her, she turned and went back.

She turned the music on, sat down, and had a very quiet lunch alone. Just as she was finishing, Zach came through the door. Desiree tried to sound pleasant,

"I made lunch for us." He went over, helped himself to a burger, ate, and went back outside.

She sat down to read her book, but could not concentrate on the story. Desiree could not wait until this day was over and was happy to be going home. She tried to make the best of a bad situation and, even thought for a moment, she would try to talk to Zach and get this straightened out. However, his body language was loud and clear; leave me alone. Therefore, she did.

Zach and Desiree made it through dinner, no candles, no sweetie can I get you anything, no conversation.

Zach turned on the television, went and took a shower and after watching a program, got up and went to bed. Desiree read for a while and decided to sleep on the sofa.

Sunday morning, Zach woke her up running around getting ready to leave. She took a shower, dressed, and packed her bag. He loaded his truck up and they left.

They went to Dave's house, where everyone seemed uncomfortable. Zach just could not stand still. Dave told him,

"Man, you need to settle down and just relax,"

Zach said,

"I can't, I have a lot to do."

He asked her to drive the car and follow him to the transmission place so he could drop off his truck. When they got there, he parked it and they jumped on the highway and headed to Indiana.

He saw a McDonalds and pulled off.

"Let's go in." They got their breakfast and sat down to eat. He tried to make small talk and she did too. She thought that maybe he is over it, as he seemed to be relaxing. They talked a little on the way home.

After a long drive, they pulled in to the driveway and home never looked so good. Zach grabbed her bag and followed Desiree into the house. As they were coming through the door, he said,

"Home sweet home." It sounded rather sarcastic and she knew he was still angry.

He went straight to the laundry room and grabbed some clean clothes that were hanging, and then started looking around the room, grabbing anything he saw that belonged to him. He turned and looked at her and said, "I guess you know it's over."

She tried to get him to sit down and talk about it,

"There is nothing to talk about," and he turned his back on her and left. Desiree could not understand why he had overreacted this time. It seemed she had touched a nerve.

She was somewhat relieved but still could not imagine why he was so angry. She had done worse things. She felt that if the situation had been reversed and she had done nothing wrong, while she might get angry, it was not enough to end a relationship over.

Desiree went upstairs to her office and sat down in front of the computer. She entered the number that was in Zach's gray box. The name and address popped up, it was a neighbor. 'But why was his line ran into Zach's box?' Maybe it was not Zach. Maybe she had overreacted.

A part of her was as relieved as much as the other part was devastated. She gathered all of his belongings and took them to the garage. She had felt crazy but within days, Desiree could feel herself calming down.

A week went by and Zach called.

"I said that I would be back to get my things but I am not coming back until after the 4th. There are many people up here, and we are going to be busy. However, don't worry, I'll take pictures."

"Take pictures of what?"

"I will take pictures of the fireworks, since you will not be here this year."

"Are you trying to upset me?"

"No, but you're not going to be here, like you usually are."

Tiring from what was beginning to feel like punishment, she remarked,

"Zach, please say hello to everyone for me, will you, goodbye."

The fireworks were on the lake up there on July 2nd. It was a Friday, so she made up her mind; she would just keep busy visiting with her friends or going shopping.

The first thing she did was to get a new doorknob so she could change the locks. As she was heading to her car, Desiree ran into an old girlfriend so they stopped and chatted. She seemed curious,

"Do you know Cheryl Dunlap?"

"No I don't."

"She works with me at the middle school and I heard her talking to another teacher about Zach. Apparently, her mother-in-law is a friend of his; they have a place on the lake in Wisconsin. She said he is a jerk, thinks he is God's gift to women and he treated his wife terribly."

"Well, we are not seeing each other, so I guess that it doesn't matter."

They caught up on other things, promised to get together soon, and she left. Desi went home and changed the locks. She felt strong and confident that they were truly over this time.

On Saturday the 3rd, Abby was having a party and invited her to come. She hopped in her car and stopped by the gas station to fill up the tank when her cell phone rang. It was Zach. He still seemed angry,

"I want my stuff."

"Okay, when do you want it?"

"Right now."

"Where are you?" she asked.

"I'm in your driveway."

"I thought you said you would not be back until next week?"

"So what, I am here, can I get my things?"

"I will be there in a few minutes."

Desiree pulled in the drive and there were people everywhere. The girl in the town home in her complex and the one next door were having a party. Everyone was going back and forth with chairs all over her driveway.

She got out of the car, went over to his truck, and asked him to come in. "I just want to get my things and go."

"Zach as you can see there is a party going on out there. Some of those people are clients of mine, could you please wait until tomorrow."

"Okay, can I at least get my duffle bag?"

"Sure."

They walked to the garage. He got his duffle bag, threw it in his truck, and followed her back in. They were talking and Desiree asked him if he knew Cheryl Dunlap. He never answered the question, he just asked why.

"She's saying things about you."

"Sweetie, you are going to hear things, just ignore it."

He said he had many parties to go to, got in his truck and left. He came by the next morning, loaded up his truck, and came to the door to say goodbye.

Chapter 23

Zach seemed to be angry but Desiree thought it was because he was simply too stubborn to say,

"I overreacted, I'm sorry."

She was determined to move forward and kept as busy as possible. She went over to Ken and Shelly's house that night to watch the fireworks and have a cookout. It was a nice evening with friends; she knew she would be okay.

Jett came from Indianapolis to spend the following weekend; Jake and Desiree always looked forward to seeing him. On Saturday out of the blue, Zach called.

"I wanted to check on you and make sure you are alright."

"Zach I am always going to be okay." The conversation lasted two hours.

He seemed unsure of his decision but Desiree was still okay with it. She knew that after all of these years she wanted more than she was ever going to get out of this relationship. He called again a few days later and made small talk and, while she enjoyed the call, she was confident it was over.

They spent the weekend with Jett catching up on everything that was going on in his life, and as always, they hated to see Sunday come.

Tuesday morning, and it was back to work once again. Overall, she was feeling good.

As Desiree was taking her usual route to work, she rounded the corner, headed for the stoplight at the intersection of Highway 30, an historic highway that stretched from one coast to the other. As she turned on her signal to make a right turn she could not help but notice the big white pick-up truck parked at the local bar on the corner.

The Texan Pipeline was an old bar in a ramshackle building that stuck out like a sore thumb now that there were new homes and businesses going up all around. The area was growing rapidly, and soon this place would be gone and a Walgreen's in its place.

It was 8:30 am and there was Zach's truck strategically parked so anyone driving by would see the license plate indicating the owner was from Wisconsin. The bar was not open, but Robert, a well-known small business owner in the area and an acquaintance of his, was usually there early to do the banking, stock shelves or fix whatever needed fixing, from the night before.

Robert had a place on the lake that Zach had been going to for years. Desiree justified it and kept driving, after all, he had a right to be there, it was a public place. However, morning after morning that truck became a regular sight. She tried to ignore it but she could not help but wonder what he was trying to say by doing this.

Jake was on summer break and asked if she would drop him off at his best friend's house. Tad had been Jake's friend since they met in pre-school. His family was more than welcoming when Jake came to visit.

Their family consisted of Jake and Desiree now that Jason and Jett were out of college and on their own. Jason was married and Jett was living in Indianapolis with his long time girlfriend. Therefore, Jake was all she had.

Desiree could see that he was outgrowing their games of Scrabble, Yahtzee, and her lame attempts at playing soccer and hockey with him. Tad's family consisted of a mom and dad so Desiree wanted him exposed to this kind of situation, as well as to theirs.

They left early and were approaching the intersection, expecting to see Zach's truck sitting in its usual spot. Desiree glanced in her rear view mirror so she could move to the right lane to turn, when she saw Zach barreling toward the intersection in the left lane.

Before she reached the corner, he passed them, honking his horn, waving while turning in to the parking lot at the same time. Jake said, "Hey, Mom! There's Zach."

"Oh I see him," and continued. 'Great job,' she thought.

All day she tried to concentrate but her mind kept trying to decipher what he was trying to do. Part of Desiree felt the situation was a little creepy while her heart wanted to believe he loved her so much, he just could not stay away. This pattern would soon become all too familiar.

Darlene, a client and friend, had apparently become fast friends with Zach. She still called from time to time but their conversations were different. She would let her know when Zach stopped by and how they talked about their dogs, how he helped rearrange her furniture, and repaired whatever needed repaired.

One morning Zach called the salon asking if he could come in around 1 o'clock for a haircut. Desiree agreed and he came in with an armload of fresh vegetables, reminding her of when they first met.

He was wearing that killer smile as he laid the veggies on her desk and came back to the shampoo area. "I only want my neck trimmed and my hair cut around my ears."

As she was cutting his hair, he did most of the talking. The haircut took only a few minutes and as a regular client would do, he paid and headed for the door. She followed him to the parking lot, making small talk as they went.

Desiree stopped as he continued to his truck, still talking as he went, his back to her and when he reached the door, she yelled,

"Hey!" He slowly turned to face Desiree and as he smiled, and she smiled back asked, "Before you go............. Do you wanna dance?"

"Where do you want to dance to, Sweetie?"

With that, she smiled as he got in his truck, and she turned to go back inside. When she reached the door she looked back, and he was gone. She went on with her day and just before closing, the phone rang. It was Zach.

"If you ever want to go out for a drink, just call me."

Darlene called too, letting her know that her friend, neighbor, and an old client of Desiree's, had passed away from breast cancer; she had suffered for a long time, and although she had been a fighter, she had lost her battle.

She promised to call with the arrangements when she got them. "Oh by the way,

Zach was here today."

"Yes, he was here too, he came over and had his haircut."

"He didn't mention it."

"No, and he probably didn't mention that he has been sitting on the corner by my house almost every morning either."

"I'll have to ask him about that."

She was listening to this in total disbelief. Was something going on between them? She was at least fifteen years older than he was and although she was single, retired, and attractive for her age, she did not think Darlene was his type. It all seemed ludicrous to her.

Zach had become seemingly indispensable to Darlene, repairing things, making conversation and even helping her rearrange furniture. She added,

"You really need to let him go."

"Darlene does Zach tell you, he is still calling me, and asking me out? He left your house today, got his hair barely trimmed, and then went back to your house as though nothing happened."

She realized that reacting was making her look liked an obsessed girlfriend who just could not let go. Desiree ended their friendship that day and did not look back.

True friends are priceless but Darlene was now under Zach's spell and no longer a friend of hers. Zach seemed to have the ability to turn people's heads inside out and did so with such grace.

In the meantime, Desiree was making plans to go to Siesta Key, the paradise island she had discovered, and that was now her sanctuary. She spent endless hours feeling the powder, white sand between her toes, watching the white caps roll to the shore, the birds glide in and out, smelling the salt in the air, and making sure, she was there to watch the sun set over the horizon. This place made Desiree feel whole, peaceful and at home.

Jake and work were her responsibility. Grace had taught her that making a living and taking care of your children to the best of your ability were your first priorities. Men stopped being her priority when John died and she did the best she could with her children. Desiree was determined to make sure her children had more love, attention, and education than she did.

Zach called wanting to talk before she left. They met for dinner where he told her he loved her and wanted them back together.

"I need time to think, this time," and she promised to consider it while she was gone.

Boarding the plane, she left it all behind. Desiree was looking forward to her destination, the only place that she could be and feel safe, just waking, taking it all in, no responsibilities, and taking care of only her. The days flew by and before she knew it, she was boarding the plane back to reality, smog, traffic jams, unpredictable weather, and where people's attitudes were just as unpredictable.

Zach and Desiree got back together without a conversation, as though they had not been apart. He seemed happy while Desiree felt a little skeptical. He called the day after she returned to let her know what he was doing and what time he would be home. Unexpectedly, she said,

"You and I both know you have been dating."

She did not know where this question came from. It was as if her conscious mind had become so weak, that her subconscious mind had taken over. Desiree never knew when this would happen and was always as surprised as he was when she blurted them out.

"You didn't think I was just sitting around doing nothing, did you?"

She was stunned, "Who have you been seeing?"

"Brenda Stiller."

"Zach, I have been dealing with this Brenda Stiller thing for two years now!" After finding her number under his loveseat and later in his spiral notebook, she was done.

"Well you didn't want me. We were friends, and I thought why not?"

At the time she found the numbers, he explained they were just friends. She was 52 years old, 5'2", and 150 pounds. He was 48 at the time and she could not imagine him throwing it all away for that, but there they were two years later and he was dating her. She ended it before it started, still wondering if she was too suspicious, too jealous, and extremely insecure, as he would often tell her.

Back at work, where she was most comfortable, she was laughing and talking to her client, who like many of them, had become her friend.

"Lars, I guess Zach is dating someone from Wisconsin."

"I know."

"How do you know?"

"I promised I would not tell."

It had to be Sandy. She had just seen her and she was telling her about the girl she worked with who knew Zach. She did not have good things to say about him. She asked Lars if her suspicions were correct and he admitted they were. "

She was drunk. I saw her at a bar in town, and she told me but did not want me to tell you where it came from."

"Well, Zach already told me, its okay."

Sandy told her later that Cheryl had said,

"Zach brought a lady who had worked with him at Lowes to the lake to watch fireworks. He spoke to her as if she were a dog. I would have told him to get screwed and left. He thinks he's God's gift to women!"

Zach began calling Jake on his cell phone after 8 pm, which just happened to be when she got home from work. One night Jake was talking on his phone and not paying much attention Desiree went up to her room, as she always did. She always shed her clothes, took a long hot bath, and put her lounging clothes on, which could consist of a nice gown all the way to sweats or a long tee shirt, depending on the mood and who was home.

She heard a rap on her bedroom door,

"Mom, Zach wants to talk to you."

She cracked the door and took the phone.

"Hello."

"Hey, how's it going?"

"Good, what's up?"

"I bought Erik's cottages." He had told her not long ago, he would own Erik's cottages before it was over. 'How does he do this?' She thought and then remembered how he had become indispensable to Darlene and how she had turned on her like a snake. Desiree began to observe their relationship and their interaction.

Erik was in his thirties, good looking, divorced, and had a little girl. He had more money than common sense. He owned the Marina, many cottages at the lake, one Burger King and was thinking of buying another.

Erik liked to party and had many DUIs to prove it. Desiree noticed Zach becoming friendlier to him, despite the negative things he said about him. He was always at the Marina working on something and without a license; Erik began to depend on him to take him places. Zach was at his disposal.

Zach told her about a conversation he had with Erik.

"You have too much pressure on you, with the Burger Kings, the Marina, and all of your cottages; you need to get rid of something."

Before you knew it, he was selling the cottages and Zach was right there to take them off his hands. 'Imagine that,' she thought.

He already had plans to build more. He also had the house he had bought in Highland to remodel and sell; he was a busy man indeed, and still juggling.

In the summer of 2006, he had moved back in with Desiree and Jake. Jake was delighted; he had missed him.

She felt, the times they were apart, he had the right to date whomever he wanted; after all, they were not together. Nevertheless, it did not keep her from asking Zach if he had sex with Brenda. He said no, they had made out on his sofa but that was it. She felt he was obligated to tell her. Desiree had lived too long to contract an STD and she did not know Brenda or her past.

This bothered Desiree for days, two adults who were obviously attracted enough to each other to date and they only made out? When he came home one evening, he sat at the dining table to visit while Jake was out playing soccer with his friends. She was preparing dinner and they were talking.

Out of nowhere, she asked,

"Do you consider oral sex, sex?"

Startled by the question, he looked up from the newspaper, above the top of his reading glasses,

"What?"

"Do you consider oral sex, sex?"

He did not pause,

"No."

Desiree thought, 'He is going to use the Bill Clinton defense.' "I did not have sex with that woman."

"Did you have oral sex with Brenda?"

This was the first time Desiree actually saw the reaction she now knew as 'the deer in the headlights look.' His neck became elongated, his eyes were wide and fixed, and his skin changed color to a pale gray. He had a fixed stare and remained quiet.

"You did, didn't you?"

After staring and being seemingly appalled at the question, he answered,

"She did with me."

She was furious.

"Now I know why you don't want to be married, Zach. Why would you when you can have sex here and in Wisconsin!"

Chapter 24

Desiree asked him to leave, and he did but within a couple of weeks, he was back. The day after he moved his clothes in, her best friend, Abby, came by for a haircut. She seemed to have something on her mind, and it was not long before Desi found out what it was.

"Des, I hate to be the one to tell you this, but Dale told Carolyn, Zach was out with another girl at Angelo's last week."

Feeling deflated she said, "Abby, I just let him move his clothes back in."

"Just take a little advice from your best friend. Do not trust your bartender friend, she is not telling you everything he does."

Desiree walked over to the phone and dialed Zach's number.

"Hey baby, what's going on?"

"I am finished at the salon, I'm coming up there." He was working on the house in Highland.

"I'm coming that way, I'll just stop by the shop." Before Abby and Desiree finished talking, Zach was there. Abby greeted him, gave Desiree a hug and left.

"Is there something wrong?" he asked

"I'll talk to you when we get home." As he walked out to head home, he playfully said, "I'll race yah!" She closed the salon and went home. He was there when she arrived.

Desiree went upstairs and Zach was lying on his back on the bed running his hands through his hair. Where had she seen that before?

They did not talk that night but Desiree began to think about the spiral notebook and the last entry, with the name Yancy and her cell phone number.

Several weeks earlier, he had left it lying open on the kitchen table.

She could not sleep so Desiree got up, went to his truck, and got his briefcase. She did not have a clue what she was looking for. She pulled out another case, which held his business cards. He had quite a collection; neatly displayed in a folder. She had no idea what she expected to find. It was as though someone else had taken over her mind.

As she was going through them, she noticed one card in particular, New Dimensions Salon. 'Why does he have a business card to a salon in this folder?'

She pulled it out wondering when he would wake up and catch her going through his personal things. This was so out of character for her, but she was becoming someone she did not even know, and she did not like her very much either.

Desiree turned the card over and in handwriting she did not recognize, was the name Yancy and a cell phone number. She hurriedly put it back and took the briefcase back to his truck, trying to remember the exact position that she had found it in. This is much harder to do than she thought. You have to be conscious about everything at all times when you are investigating. If she were not so upset, this would be funny. Desiree would laugh someday, but not that day.

The next night they were lying on her bed and grasping at straws, she asked,

"Do you know anyone named Yancy?"

"Yancy, hmmm let me see, I just know Jeanette's friend, Yancy, why?"

"Is she a hairstylist?"

"No."

Thinking about the piece of paper she found with the name Terry on it, as well as her number, "Do you know a girl named Terry?"

"No I don't."

"You don't know a hairstylist named Yancy, who works at New Dimensions Salon?"

"No, why do you ask?"

Desiree now knew he was lying, but he was not going to admit it. Zach was leaving in the morning and she needed time to think about what to do while he was gone.

She could not accuse him of being with either one of them because she had no proof and this time she wanted to be sure.

The following day, Friday Zach was supposed to ride with Benny to Wisconsin and come home the following week with Al. Zach decided they were going to wait until Saturday to leave; he had too much to do to leave that day.

Desiree thought this was odd, he usually jumped at the chance to go hunting with his friends, but she let it go. The day was uneventful; it was the end of the week and she was looking forward to the weekend. She needed a break.

On Saturday, Zach left at the same time she did. She noticed he had not packed to leave but she did not say a word, she just went on to work.

He called her later and when she asked what time he was leaving, he said, "Oh, we decided to wait until tomorrow."

She was supposed to go to the Quest with Mariah, but when she called, Desiree explained that plans had changed; Zach had decided to leave on Sunday. Desiree told her she would go with her Sunday afternoon.

The next morning, Zach went to the Highland house and she got up, got dressed, and took Jake to his soccer game.

Desiree called him from the soccer arena,

"When are you leaving?"

"Not until tomorrow."

She tried to act surprised,

"I'm stopping by the store, do you need anything?"

"A bag of money." This answer was no longer funny. She soon came to realize this was not a joke; he meant it.

Now she knew something was wrong and while he was gone, she was going to get to the bottom of it.

Chapter 25

On Monday morning, her day off, Zach got up, packed his bag, kissed Desiree good-bye, and left for Benny's house. He was finally going hunting and she could now focus on what to do.

He called her several times when he arrived, and many more after that. When he was hunting, he usually only called at night.

With every call, he convinced her something was wrong and that made Desiree more suspicious than ever. Desiree was getting ready to cross another line she had never crossed before. She decided she was definitely going to New Dimensions Salon before the week was over.

She went back to work on Tuesday, it was a slow day so she decided to run up to Highland. She wanted to get a better printer for the salon, so she went to Office Depot.

While she was comparing prices, her phone rang. "Hey baby what are you doing and where are you?"

"I'm at Office Depot looking at printers, there are so many I'm confused. Maybe I'll just wait until you come home so you can help me decide."

There seemed to be a sound of relief in his voice. Desiree could almost hear him exhale,

"Sure sweetie I can do that." She had begun to doubt herself about confronting this situation until that call. Now she knew she had to. She left the store and headed back to the salon.

It was a cold crisp day but it was mild compared to the winters, she had experienced as a child. Desiree's mind drifted back to when things were much simpler. They had mounds of snow all winter long and bitter cold temperatures as well. The snow seemed like mountains back then, just as the roads seemed to stretch on forever.

Desiree remembered their house was enormous with a long, driveway. She remembered frozen tag, Mother may I, Statues, Red Rover, Red Rover and, Fly's up. She could see it like it was yesterday. She laughed at the memory of Katy and her best friend, Sheila performing for the neighbor boys. They danced and did a lip-sync to Lollipop, Lollipop, she had been the stage manager. She remembered walking on barrels down a huge hill in the front yard. Desiree was thinking of how coordinated she must have been to be able to keep that barrel under control and remain on it.

She smiled as she reminisced. She began thinking about when she drove passed the house where she grew up. Going back, she turned on 45th Street, remembering it as a long drive to her childhood home, but she had just turned when she passed their old house.

Desiree turned around in what used to be their childhood friends' driveway. There were seven boys in that family, even one named Jimbo. Every girl's dream, she had thought as a child. The house was no longer there but the memories were still fresh in her mind.

She pulled in her old driveway and was astounded at how short it was and how close their house was to the street. 'They must have moved it,' she thought, noticing they had added on to the upstairs.

The big hill in the front was no more than a barely recognizable slope. The huge oak tree on the edge of the yard was gone; the one there now was much smaller than she remembered.

Next door had been a cornfield and their tire swing hung from the huge oak tree. That is where she spent, what seemed like hours, trying to swing as high as she could over the field. She felt as if she was flying and sometimes she wished she could. Desiree was a little girl who always wanted her feet firmly planted on the ground. She was afraid of anything that took her feet off the ground, and yet for some reason, she loved the rocking motion when she was on a swing.

She would not climb trees, it took Desiree forever to learn to ride a bike, and riding horses was simply out of the question.

She always envied Katy's ability to do all of these things; her heart wished she could rid herself of that fear, but it did not happen.

When she was in her swing, she would dream of a better place, like Dorothy or meeting her Prince on a white horse, like Cinderella. Desiree knew there was more than West 45th Street.

As these memories were passing through her mind, Desiree realized she was pulling in the parking lot at the salon, and wondered how she had managed to reach her destination.

Thursday was her late day. She did not have to be at work until noon, so she would go to New Dimensions Salon. What she was going to do when she got there, she did not know but she was going.

She slept in on Thursday, leisurely taking her shower; this time it took longer to get ready. She wanted to look nice if she was going to go in another salon.

She left the house about 10:30 am wondering what she was going to do or say. Oh well, she would think of something. Desiree was becoming braver in dealing with these situations head on. She did not know where this strength came from but it was a gradual awakening.

She pulled up in what appeared to Desiree to be a new strip mall and parked the car. She walked through the door, was greeted by the receptionist and the girl behind the first chair. She instinctively knew this was Yancy.

She had blonde hair, a great body and was very pretty. She turned when Desiree came in, and smiled,

"Hello." The salon was small but nicely decorated Highland style, an upper end salon and much nicer than her place.

The receptionist asked if she could help her and as if Desiree had done this before, "Sure I would like a menu, please." As she handed one to Desiree, the woman asked what she was interested in having done.

"A highlight" she said, without skipping a beat. Looking at Yancy, she said,

"Excuse me, I know you from somewhere." Desiree recognized her but did not know from where, but she had seen her before.

She turned and asked,

"Where do you hang out?" 'I do not hang out,' danced across her mind.

"The Quest," she responded.

"I was just there last night; do you know Michael and Jen?"

"No I don't"

"That's who I hang out with."

"Your name is?"

"Yancy."

"It was nice to meet you Yancy, have a good day." She would not see Yancy again; little did she know she would come in to her life one more time. She seemed to be a genuinely nice person and after all, none of this was her fault.

Desiree went back to work and forced herself to focus on her job when Kyle came in.

Desiree had known him for years before she met Zach and they were friends.

"You look like you could use a night out, would you like to go out for a drink tonight."

"I sure would," she replied.

They arranged to meet at North Star's at 6 pm. They made small talk while she cut his hair; he hugged her as he always did and then left.

Desiree finished up at work, called Jake, and told him she was going out with a client and she would be home soon. As always, Desiree arrived early and stood in the waiting area watching for Kyle, relieved that this day was almost over.

Her phone rang, "Hey sweetie, where are you?"

"I am at North Star's, meeting a client for dinner." He was telling her about his day, when she saw Kyle coming through the door,

"I have to go, my client is here; I'll talk to you later." Kyle gave her a hug; little did he know, she really needed one and they went in to the bar. He looked up and asked,

"Are you hungry?"

"A little."

He stood up and said,

"Let's go next door to Angelo's, they have better food. You can just ride with me and I'll bring you back to your car later."

They jumped in his Jeep and made the short drive to Angelo's. Desiree knew Denise would be working but she went in any way.

Denise was now bartending there. She remembered what Abby had told her and, decided she did not care if she did tell him about her being there tonight.

Maybe she would not say anything. Bartenders, she realized, depend on tips and for bigger tips; they keep their customers' secrets. They sat in a booth, ordered and she suggested they might as well sit at the bar as Denise had already seen them come in, and she did not want to ignore her.

They moved to the bar, where Desiree introduced them. They got their steaks and while they were eating, talking, and laughing, she heard her phone ring but she ignored it. Before the evening was over it would ring three more times. They finished their dinner and ordered a drink while Denise joined in the conversation.

They were there about two hours and decided they had better go; Jake was waiting at home. Kyle drove her back to her car, kissed her, and said goodnight.

Desiree started her car, while she reached in her purse to check her phone. Zach had called several times. She was certain he had to know how suspicious this was becoming. He had been unreadable in the past, but red flags were now flying higher than ever.

She went home, made dinner for Jake, and spent some time with him before they went up to bed. Zach called at bedtime, and while he did not ask why she had not answered his calls, he seemed very interested in what she was doing.

Finally, it was Friday. It would be a short day, Mariah and Desiree had decided, since Jake would be going to his dad's for the weekend, they would go to the Quest since their plans had to be cancelled because of Zach's change of plans. Zach, surprisingly, had not called all day and she was not calling him either. She was filling Mariah in on what was going on when finally he called. "Desiree speaking, can I help you?"

"Hey sweetie, are you busy?"

"I'm with my last client. What are you doing?"

"I'm sitting here with Al. We are so tired."

"I am rinsing a client's hair and I'm busy, Can I call you back?"

"I am going to cook some eggs and we're going to bed, I'll talk to you tomorrow, I love you, goodnight."

About a half, an hour later something told her to call him back.

"Hey, I wanted you to know I'm going with Mariah to the Quest."

As though he did not hear her, he answered, "I am sitting here with Al and Erik, having a beer."

"I thought you were going to bed, did you eat?"

"No not yet, I love you, bye."

Mariah ran home to change clothes and put on some makeup, while Desiree cleaned up the salon.

They met at the Quest about 8:30 pm and immediately ordered their drinks. Other than the dinner with Kyle, due to the stress, she had hardly eaten all week and she should have known better than to drink on an empty stomach, especially in her state of mind.

After her third rum and coke, she blacked out. Desiree's cell phone rang and Mariah took it in to the bathroom to answer it. She came out, and handed her the phone. Later Mariah told her it was Zach.

Desiree vaguely remembered him saying, "Leave me alone." That is about all she remembered about the entire evening, other than a friend coming in and taking her home.

Mariah called the next day to fill her in on what happened the night before. She said, "You kept calling Zach and leaving messages and finally he called back,

"May I speak to Desiree, please?"

"Is this Andrew?"

"No."

"Tom?"

"No this is Zach, let me speak to Desiree."

Desi was immediately regretful and hoped it was just a bad dream. 'What has happened to me? Who have I become?' She barely recognized herself these days. She did not hear from him again until Tuesday night.

Zach called and said he was coming to get his things. They went upstairs and sat on her bed.

"I'm done, but before I go, I want to talk to you. First of all, I want you to listen to the messages you left on my phone."

"I don't want to listen to them."

"You should. I let Dr. Daniel listen to them, and he said to tell you, if you are going to drink, don't take pills, and if you are going to take pills, do not drink."

"Why did you let him listen to that? You know how much I think of Dr. Daniel. I can't believe you did that!"

"I was concerned about you."

"Zach you are the one who drinks Scotch everyday and are always taking pills, not me. You are everything you accuse me of, why do you do that?" He ignored the question.

"While I am here, I want you to know, I never dated Yancy, Matthew introduced her to me, and I needed a haircut."

"No you didn't Zach, we were only broken up for two weeks, and aside from that, you do not have the owner of a salon's cell phone number to make an appointment. She has a receptionist for that."

"I never went out with her, she has a boyfriend. Eighty five percent of everything you think has happened never happened."

"What about the other fifteen percent?"

"Why do you want to hurt yourself like that? Do not push me. You are always pushing. I am going to tell you what I do.

I sit in bars and I become a regular at many different ones. I get to know everyone around me. I do not give a shit if it is a man or woman; it makes no difference to me.

I wine them and dine them, I shmoo them and before you know it someone has a job for her me. I have been doing this for over 20 years. I do not have a place to work, like you do, bars are my office."

"Is that what Tara was all about, was she getting you jobs?"

"Bingo." He said.

Desiree cried as she was listening to this.

"I am used to a man going to work, putting his time in and coming home, I have never heard of such a thing!"

"Now, you have."

"How many women believe they are dating my boyfriend?"

"I don't give a shit what they think as long as I get their money. You do not date your job; it is unprofessional to mix business with pleasure. This is not going to work for us; I have too much to do. You do not trust me and I do not have time for this bullshit. There can only be one alpha-dog in this relationship."

"What is an alpha-dog?"

"It is the leader of the pack."

"There is a difference in being a leader of the pack Zach, and being a dictator."

"Maybe somewhere down the road, if we are both available, we can work this out, but not now. You need to let it go."

She did.

Chapter 26

Zach's paranoid behavior was beginning to make sense to her now. Thinking back on the time when she called him and asked where he was, and he replied,

"The Texas Corral." It was around 12:20 in the afternoon.

"I'm about to pass there," Desiree replied, expecting an invitation to stop by.

"Oh ya, what time's your first client?"

"1:00."

"Did they cancel?"

"No, why?"

"I was just wondering."

"I love you, see ya later."

"I love you too, bye."

Desiree went on to work even though she had a strong feeling that she should have stopped in. Her client was there on time. The salon phone rang it was Zach. She glanced at the clock it was 1:01.

Ten minutes after she hung up, he came walking through the door. He did not say anything; he just sat down in a waiting room chair. She continued with her client and he just sat there for about 15 minutes as though he were waiting for something. In order to clear the air that suddenly felt thick she asked,

"How was lunch?"

By this time he was getting up, "It was okay. I will see you when you get home tonight."

He left as instantly as he had appeared. Desiree could not help but think that was odd behavior. 'Why does he always seem preoccupied, or maybe paranoid is a better word,' she wondered.

Those thoughts dissipated and the tears were now running in a steady stream.

"I'm going to stay here tonight and leave first thing in the morning. It is over for now."

She slept surprisingly well that night. Desiree awoke to Jake asking her for a ride to school. It was nasty outside; it had been snowing all night.

She slipped out of bed, bundled up and snuck out of the house. She did not want to wake Zach so she had to maneuver around his truck.

As she was pulling back into the driveway, Desiree noticed the truck was gone. She went to the closet and his clothes were gone. She ran downstairs to the cabinet where he kept his Scotch, and it was gone too.

She went up stairs crying, and called him.

"You could have at least said good-bye."

"I'm not good at goodbye, Sweetie."

With that, she hung up the phone.

Late that night, around 11 o'clock, the phone rang. Desiree looked on caller id. It was Zach calling from his mom's phone.

"Hey sweetie, I just wanted to hear your voice."

The next day was Thanksgiving and he was making this so hard. Trish was in town and they had gone out to celebrate the holiday.

"I guess they know what is going on."

"They do."

They spoke for a long time and he tried to explain, but the more he tried, the crazier it sounded.

"If I wanted to be married I would want to be married to you. I just do not want to be married. I love you very much."

"I don't understand, why?"

156

"I just don't want to be married; it's just a piece of paper. Sweetie, I just called to apologize for bailing out on you like I did."

The longer they spoke, the harder Desiree cried and she told him,

"Zach, go do what you have to do, I love you, bye."

She did not hear from him for almost three months. Desiree went to Florida with Shelly to celebrate her birthday. Shelly's relationship with Ken was nearing an end. Desiree loved Ken as a brother and did not want to lose either of them, but he and Desiree had been friends for many years, he was family.

As Desiree often did, she was relaying the latest stories to one of her clients.

"I found a piece of paper with the name Terry on it. Zach said the only Terry he knew was some girl that worked for a restoration company."

He said,

"I know her; I think she's from Highland."

"Who does she work for?"

"Potters."

Surprised at his answer, "I've seen her many times but Zach has never acknowledged her when we pass her; does she drive a Cougar like mine?"

"She used to but she has a different car now."

"Does she have blonde hair?" she asked.

"Yep, she is an attractive, well dressed girl."

Desiree remembered seeing her around town all of the time. The reason she noticed her was that they drove the same car. It was the same color and it had Potters written on the door.

"He might be getting fire jobs from her. She works for a restoration company, He's quite a guy."

The holidays were rough, but they made the best of them and once New Years was over, Desiree felt she could now go on.

Desiree would not forget that easily, but the pain was letting up. Jake's birthday came and they celebrated as they always did – a pizza cookie per his request. The next evening when she came home, she noticed a brown envelope lying by the door.

She picked it up and read it. It was addressed to Jake, and was from Zach. Jake opened it and found a gift card for $50.00 from Cabelas.

The note in it read, 'Happy Birthday Jake, I hope we can go fishing very soon Love, Zach.'

Jake was elated and sent him a thank-you card. A week later, the end of January, Desiree was heading back to work after running an errand and as she approached the intersection in front of the salon, Zach passed her and honked his horn.

Desiree had not seen him since November and suddenly there he was. She had no idea why he was in town and did not want to know either. She let it go.

It was Desiree's birthday and all of her friends made sure she had a good one. Her 50th birthday – a milestone – it was a time to look back on her accomplishments, not her failures.

Friends stopped by with gifts and cards and Wayne, a client and good friend, who had sat for hours listening to the same stories repeatedly, walked in the salon carrying a dozen roses.

"Do you have a client coming in?"

"No, not for a while."

"Do you have a lunch date?"

"No, I don't."

"Now you do, let's go."

Desiree took him up on his offer and they went to a restaurant down the street. "It is nice to have friends like you."

"You'd do the same for me, it is the least I can do."

Ken called. He was having her over for dinner after work and wanted to see how her day was going.

She went straight there after work. Shelly had moved out shortly after they came back from Florida. Desiree walked in and he was busy cooking. He had set the table, and there was a rose and a card lying next to her plate.

'I am a lucky girl to have so many friends,' she thought as he was serving the stuffed grape leaves he had made. They had a glass of wine with dinner and what a way to end a great day.

Desiree went home only to find more birthday cards and as she was going through them, there was one from Zach. It looked like one you might send your grandmother. She sat it on the counter with about 20 others and went to bed.

Desiree did not respond to his card and about a week later, while cleaning house her phone rang.

"Hey, how are you?" Desiree had not heard his voice for so long; she could not believe it was Zach calling.

"I'm fine," she said cautiously.

"I bet you are cleaning aren't you? It's Monday. "I was sitting here paying my bills and was thinking of you."

"Paying bills makes you think of me?"

"No, I was just thinking of you." she tried not to make conversation. She just answered his questions.

The call was awkward and only lasted a few minutes. Another week went by and an invitation came in the mail.

It read, You are cordially, invited to attend a Birthday Party.

She opened it.

Who: Desiree Peters

When: March 14.

Where: Glenwood Oaks and a movie of your choice.

What time: 5 o'clock. R.S.V.P.

"Please call and let me know if you want to go so, if not, I can make other plans."

'Wow, he is so creative?'

Desiree thought about it all day and she called him and left a message for him to call her. He called back that evening and asked if she would go. Desiree said,

"Yes."

"Great, I'll see you on Saturday."

He called her house while she was at work on Friday and left a message, Desiree thought this was strange, as he knew she was at work.

"Hi, it's Zach, It is about 2 o'clock, Wisconsin time; I will pick you up at 4:30 tomorrow. I'm looking forward to it, bye."

Desiree convinced herself that they could go out as friends and was excited, as she was getting ready to go. The doorbell rang. She answered the door, he flashed that smile, and Desiree was happy to see him.

"You look so nice, you're dressed up, and I'm not. I was out late with Al and his train friends. I'm tired; I didn't get home until two this morning."

"When you called yesterday it sounded as though you were still in Wisconsin when you said, it's 2 o'clock Wisconsin time." Desiree found out later he had seen one of her clients the previous night and knew she would find out.

She let it go when he did not respond. She was going out for a nice dinner that he was paying for; and tried to convince herself she did not care.

Conversation came easy to them; they had their server take a picture of them to mark the occasion. When they went to the movies, there was nothing good playing. Desiree suggested they go to the movie rental store, pick up a movie, and go back to her place. They did not find any that they liked so they went back to her house to see what was on HBO.

They went up to her room and while they were trying to find a movie they both liked, Desiree excused herself and went to the bathroom. When she came out, she was carrying her backscratcher trying to reach an itch.

"What are you doing?"

"I'm trying to scratch my back."

"Take your top off and get the lotion, I'll do it."

It seemed so natural and innocent and she complied.

When he was finished, she put her top back on and went back to surfing the channels. He said, "My back itches too." By this time, Desiree could see right through his manipulation.

"I'll put lotion on you too." He stood up and pulled his shirt off.

Oh no, not that, she thought as Desiree tried not to notice his hairy, lean chest. He lay on his belly and she rubbed the lotion in, when he suddenly he rolled over on his back so she could get his chest. Desiree slathered it on as quickly as possible, it was a little more than she could handle.

She did not take the time to rub it in and went back to channel surfing. He looked at his watch,

"What time is it? I better go." He got up and she let him.

Desiree immediately walked downstairs ahead of him. They talked, she told him how she felt about some of the things that had gone on during their relationship, and gave him the Christmas presents she had already purchased before they broke up.

"Zach, I just want you to know, that I know some of those blocked calls I got came from you. I heard the beep of your watch on one of the calls. When you called me at home that time, while I was at work and Tim was at the cabin, you simply forgot to press star 67 before the call. You were trying to convince me that Sheila was calling so I would not contact Tara." He said nothing and continued to stare.

"Zach, I don't know why you did that. Were you trying to avoid confrontation?" "Yes."

Desiree was upset with herself for giving him another out.

He thanked her for the evening and left. In some ways, she was proud of herself. She did not cave in, and was indeed getting stronger. It was good to see him and much easier to see him leave.

Chapter 27

On Tuesday morning, she had an appointment with her attorney. Dan was not paying Jake's medical bills and once again, she would have to take him to court to get them paid.

While she was there, she had planned to ask for more child support. The $50 per week he was paying had never been enough and now seemed ridiculous.

Dan had remarried and had a daughter. He lived in a beautiful house and bragged all over town about his success. In the meantime, Desiree was struggling to make sure Jake had no clue that she was struggling.

As she was waiting for her turn, her cell phone rang.

"Hi, Zach how are you?"

"I was wondering if you could fit me in for a haircut today."

"I thought you went back to Wisconsin."

"I'm leaving tomorrow, can you fit me in?" he asked again.

"I'm at my attorney's office."

"Oh, I'm sorry. I'll call you later."

"Okay, bye."

The attorney agreed. Dan was in contempt of court and an increase in support was long overdue. She went straight from there to work and began her day.

As Zach had promised, he called back and made an appointment for that evening at six pm. Six o'clock came quickly, Zach seemed to be in a hurry, looking at the clock on the wall and his watch often.

They had a friendly conversation; he remarked on the outfit she was wearing, as he liked it. Funny how when they were not together, he loved her hair, her outfits, but when they were together, she needed a new haircut and her jeans did nothing for her. 'Amazing' she thought. He did not linger long; he said he had somewhere to be.

He called the salon within minutes of leaving.

"Go outside." Desiree went outside and stood in the parking lot.

"Look up at the moon; isn't it beautiful."

"It sure is."

"I will talk to you later." She shook her head and went back inside.

She was researching online for equipment for the new salon she had envisioned. Desiree was determined to do whatever it took to make sure this was over for them. She knew if she went head over heels in debt, it would force her to focus on something other than Zach. Jake was not coming to the salon anymore and being there to raise him had served its purpose; it was time for a change.

Because she loved going to the beach, Desiree decided she would surround herself with all things to do with it. She got excited about her new adventure and threw herself in to it.

She was negotiating another store in the same mall. Desiree was online comparing prices on equipment and décor. She was taking care of Jake, and consumed with anything that would prevent her from going through this pain again.

Zach called a few days after he returned to Wisconsin to offer his help with the new salon. Desiree declined and reminded him she had all of the help she needed. He began calling to see how she was doing and how the salon was progressing.

Desiree suddenly had more energy, and was sure of what she was doing. Everything seemed to be falling in place. Wayne was there every day offering his help and she appreciated it very much.

She had many offers for help and turned some of them down. Desiree found, just like too many women working together, the same was true for men. They disagreed on just about everything. They would come in, tear down what the previous guy had done, and redo it their way.

She woke up early and was on her way to see what Wayne was up to at the salon. She knew he would already be there working hard on something. On her way, she checked her messages; it was Zach.

"Hi, Sweetie, no I am not drunk, it is 3 am, and I can't sleep. I know you will not believe this but I watched Oprah today and I think I figured it out. I am afraid of commitment."

Desiree laughed and said aloud to herself, "No kidding." She went on with her day wondering when he would realize it was over for them.

He called again several times, some of the calls lasted for hours at a time. He seemed to be sorry about the break up, as he had been many times before. She was not buying it this time.

It was the middle of April, just before Easter and although she was keeping busy, he still managed to creep into her thoughts.

Zach made an appointment for Friday to have his haircut, but on Wednesday he called, "Hey I am coming in a day early bringing my tools, do you need any help?"

"Help is not what I need from you."

"Listen, I could have Brenda back anytime I want her and, I could be with someone else, but I want to be with you. What exactly do you need from me?"

Desiree excused herself from her client, went into the restroom, and impatiently asked, "Listen Zach, do you have a suit, a ring, and a date?"

In an almost shy and pathetic voice that sounded more like a question than a comment, he said,

"I have a suit." 'His trusty blue suit' she imagined. He looked good in it and he knew it.

"Well you need to buy a ring and put it in the pocket of your suit and bring a minister with you."

"Will you have dinner with me?"

"I don't know, Zach."

"Please, I need to talk to you."

"When?"

"I will see you tomorrow at six."

"Okay, Zach goodbye."

He was on time, and suggested they go to Dick's Restaurant. They went into the bar and asked for their favorite booth in the back corner. They liked the atmosphere there. The bar was large, dimly lit and the food was good as well. They sat opposite each other and he was just staring at her. They had not done this in a long time and it always amazed her how comfortable it felt, as though they had never been apart.

The server came, they ordered their drinks, and since they usually ordered the same thing, the chicken snack, they went ahead and ordered. They were catching up on each other's lives.

It seemed like in no time their drinks and food was there. They continued talking during dinner, and Desiree looked up at him and said,

"We're talking about everything except what we came here to talk about."

"Don't worry we will, let's have dinner first." The server came, cleared the table, and asked if they needed another drink. They ordered one more and after she had brought them, he reached across the table and took her hand.

She looked up, only to see a very serious look cross his face. He announced,

"I want to get married."

"Don't lie to me."

"I'm not lying to you, I want to spend the rest of my life with you, and I promise to be true to you until the day I die. Will you marry me?"

"Yes I will."

"Sweetie there is only one catch."

'Here we go,' she thought, Desiree knew there was a catch.

"What?"

"I just bought the cottages and this is the first summer, you're starting your new business and if you will wait five months Sweetie, I will marry you any time after Labor Day."

Desiree leaned back in the booth. She needed to think. The red flag was waving, but this is what she really wanted and after all, that was not long considering they had been together for seven years already.

Zach could read Desiree like a book and saw the question in her mind,

"Sweetie it's only five months, it will go by quickly."

Desiree smiled, jumped up, and slid in next to him. She kissed him and said,

"Okay."

"I know that you want a ring about the size of this candle, and you can have one, but we won't be able to go on vacations."

With that, he looked at her and said in an irritated voice,

"You know I am not happy about doing it this way, I wanted to be on one knee and for it to be more romantic than this. I almost feel like I am being railroaded."

She ignored that last comment and smiled,

"Let's make it the Saturday after Labor Day."

"Whatever you want, baby."

"Did anyone know that you were going to do this?"

"My mom knows. I had a long talk with her two or three times and she thought it was a great idea. She's happy about it." They hurried home so they could spread the news.

Zach said,

"Let me handle this with Jake, I want to tell him. I love Jake. He's the son I never had." Desiree went upstairs to put on her sweats; Zach wanted to have a fire in the fireplace on the patio, so she planned to take her bath later.

Desiree came downstairs. Jake had the widest grin on his face, he came over and wrapped his arms around her and said he was happy for her and that he was finally going to be a part of a family.

Zach was on the phone talking to his mother,

"Well Mom, it looks like we have a new addition to the family. Desiree and I are getting married."

She was not surprised but sent her congratulations. He hung up and began calling his friends. He set up times to meet with them; he wanted to tell them in person.

Friday night Zach wanted to take Jake to Culver's for dinner. They went in, ordered their food, and sat down in a booth by the window. It was a nice sunny day and everyone was relaxed and happy. Just as they were beginning to eat, Zach's phone rang.

"Hello...hello..." He hung up the phone. As soon as he did, it started ringing again.

"Zach, why don't you take that call outside?" She no more than had got the last syllable out and he was up and on his way out the door. He was only out there for a minute before he sat back down.

"That was Erik. He wants some excavating done."

She had not asked but let it go. They finished their meal, went home for a quiet evening of television, and went to bed early.

On Saturday, Zach went to his friend Al's to deliver the news.

He called Desiree and announced,

"Babe, Al is lying on the ground right now."

"Why?"

"He passed out when I told him we were getting married. He said congratulations, I'll be home soon."

"Okay sweetie, I'll see you soon, I love you too, bye."

He came in and went straight in to take a shower. He had also stopped by to tell Matthew that they were getting married.

"He asked me, what made you decide to get married? " I told him I am tired of chasing."

"What, who or what were you chasing?"

"That is just a figure of speech, guy talk."

As he was undressing to jump in the shower, he laughed,

"You should have heard Lisa scream. Matthew called her from his cell to give her the news and she was screaming. You could hear her across the room. She said congratulations, she is happy for us too."

She could not get that phone call from the previous night off her mind. 'Does he not realize that leaving the phone in his truck is a red flag that even I cannot ignore?' He had a very bad habit of leaving his phone in the truck on the charger.

He went in to take a shower. Here she was, finally getting married and, Desiree had a nagging feeling about the call from the previous evening. She went out to see if Erik had called him the night before. She scrolled through and there it was – Jen. She scrolled a little farther and there was Julianna.

'Who are Jen and Julianna? Here we go again.' They were not together at the time, and he was free to date whomever he wanted, 'so why was he lying?'

Desiree came in, and as she walked into her bedroom, he was standing there as naked as the day he was born. He flopped down on the bed and she sat down on the floor.

"Were you dating anyone?"

"Yes, two people."

"What are their names?"

"Jen and Julianna."

"Did one of them call you last night while we were at Culver's?"

"Jen did and I told her it was over and that I was getting married." Therefore, it was not Erik and Desiree could not help but think, 'is this why he came a day early?

He probably had a date with Jen last night and did not cancel it just in case I said no to his proposal.'

He was upfront when she asked him. "Did you have sex with either of them?"

"Why do you ask questions like that?"

"I don't know these women; I want to know if I should be concerned about getting a disease."

"I had sex with Julianna from Wisconsin, not with Jen from Highland. I only went out with her a couple of times. She wasn't for me."

'Convenient' she thought, 'my, that is funny you have only been here twice since we split up and you went out with Jen a couple of times. That must have been why you were in a hurry to leave after your haircut.' At least he was telling the truth, maybe she had been wrong before. 'Over thinking again?'

"Did you have feelings for either of them?"

"Julianna, from Wisconsin."

"What does she do for a living?"

"She doesn't work, she is retired."

"How old is she?"

"About 48."

"She doesn't work, what did she do?"

Once again, the deer in the headlights look. "It's none of your business."

"Why won't you tell me what she does for a living?"

"Because, it's simply none of your business, and it doesn't matter."

Desiree struck a nerve and could not help but wonder what Julianna did that was such a secret.

"She called me shortly after you and I broke up, so I went back to Wisconsin." "We only dated for a month, from December until January.

"You and I broke up the end of November, you started dating the beginning of December and she just happened to call you a week after we split up?"

"She saw me out one night with Erik, she asked him for my number. He called to make sure it was okay to give it out and I said, yes, why not?"

"Why did you break up?"

"She was weird, she never wanted to go anywhere, or do anything."

"How did it end?"

"I called her and she never called me back."

"If she was so weird Zach, why did you keep calling her?"

"Are you going to be able to put this behind you, none of this matters?"

"I thought that you might have gone back to Brenda."

"Sweetie I have only talked to her once, and she called me."

"What did she want?"

"She asked me to go look at some houses she wanted to purchase."

"Is she moving?"

"No, she was looking for rental property."

'That is convenient,' she thought. 'If she had rental property, he could remodel them for her.' A pattern was beginning to form. 'Tara got him jobs too.' He had told Desiree that he knew Tara wanted to date him. 'But did he string her along for four years, to get jobs? That is ridiculous; he is not that good looking.'

Zach was right, if they were getting married, she had to let it go, and she did not mention it again. She could not fall asleep so she went downstairs and just sat on the sofa and stared into space.

A few minutes later, she heard Zach coming down the stairs. He curled up next to her and in a soft voice asked if she was okay. As she silently cried, she assured him she was and would be up soon. He gently kissed her and went up to bed.

The next day they began looking at rings and set the date for September 9, 2006. It was only five months away and even though they were going to the beach to be married, there was a lot to do.

Desiree had to make their reservations, get their flights, their rings, her dress. She was so excited she could hardly contain herself. Zach seemed happy to see her happy and as most guys do, went along with most of her decisions.

Chapter 28

Zach stayed with her for three weeks and it was almost time for him to go back to Wisconsin; he had a lot to do. On Sunday, they went to watch Christian play indoor soccer. While they were waiting for his game to start, Desiree heard someone yell from a distance, "Hey Zach what are you doing here?" He looked around and said, "I am watching her grandson's soccer game." She thought, 'Haven't I graduated from her, by now.' She was blonde, plain and appeared to be in her late thirties.

Who is that?"

"She rides the train with Al. Remember when I worked on that garage in Hammond? It was hers."

Al had get-togethers with people on the train about once a month. They would go to different bars. Zach was usually invited; however, Desiree had never joined them. How nice, she thought of Al to include Zach. She thought nothing much of it until they got home. Zach seemed edgy and kept trying to call Al.

"You are just dying to tell Al about the girl from the train, aren't you?" He did not respond and stopped trying to reach him that night.

The morning before he left, he got a call from one of his friends at the lake, Sylvia. She had been married to Mitchell for over 20 years, and they had a place next door to Zach's ex-wife, Sheila's cottage.

Zach always seemed envious of Mitchell. He told Desiree Sylvia had a lot of money and that Mitchell was just going along for the ride. He said, "All he does is lay around, smoke pot; boy he lives the good life."

Desiree never saw Zach or any of his friends do any drugs. He had told Desiree that those days were behind him; he had done it when he was younger but had finally outgrown it.

Zach answered his phone, "Hey, what's going on?"

"I just called to see how you were doing, who are you dating now?"

Desiree could hear everything she was saying; Zach had the volume up high for some reason.

"I'm with Desiree."

"When did that happen?"

"About three weeks ago and as a matter of fact we're getting married."

"Why are you doing that?"

He must have turned the volume down because she could no longer hear a word she said.

"Because she wants to," he replied.

Desiree continued making breakfast and setting the table as though everything was fine. 'She does not know me and has overstepped her bounds,' she thought. 'What she says has no bearing on whether we get married, just another nosy person, probably not happy in her own life and has to stick her nose in someone else's business.'

They spent the day together and she hated to see him leave but that was part of the deal and she did not mention it.

The next morning, before Zach left, Desiree asked him if she found a ring for a certain amount could she get it. She was disappointed that they had not already purchased one. They had had three weeks, but he wanted Desiree to shop around. He said yes and, being able to shop for her ring softened the blow of him leaving.

He called more often than usual and referred to himself as her future husband, which wiped away any fears that he might change his mind.

Suddenly, his moods began to change and it was obvious he was trying to create conflict.

On Saturday evening, he seemed to be distant when he called. "Where are you?" she asked.

"I'm at Barns with Erik."

"Why are you at the Marina at 10 o'clock, it's passed your bedtime?"

"It's going to be a late night; Erik's having a party and asked me to come. There's going to be a lot of people here and I have no idea when I will be home."

Desiree could sense the defiance in his voice but she did not challenge him.

"Well, if you get home early enough, call me, otherwise I'll talk to you in the morning." She went to bed knowing he was not going to call.

Desiree tossed and turned until about 3 am and finally decided she would not be able to sleep until she spoke with him.

She called and called. He did not answer, and by morning, Desiree was beside herself with worry. Not so much that he was okay but what he was doing. He had acted so strangely on the phone the night before.

Finally, about 10 am he called and said he spent the night in one of his cottages. He drank too much, and it was late so he had just stayed there.

The next night it was the same thing again. He did not call all day and when he did, he sounded as though he was angry with Desiree.

"What is wrong?" she asked.

"Nothing, it is pouring rain so hard, I can hardly see where I am driving. I am coming back from one of my cottages. I was invited to a cook out with one of my renters."

"If it's raining so hard you can barely see to drive, how did you have a cook out?"

"Well, we did."

"How did you eat in the rain?"

173

"We ate in the cottage."

She knew this conversation was futile; it was obvious he was instigating an argument so she dropped it and tried to change the subject.

He continued,

"I was talking to a guy today; he asked how old I was. When I told him, he said, Why in the hell are you getting married at your age? I'm having second thoughts."

"Zach, don't tell me a month before we are due to get married that you've changed your mind. I want to know now, before I make any more plans."

"I'm home and I'm tired, I'll talk to you later, bye." and he hung up the phone.

She dialed his number and when he answered, she said, "You can't just hang up like that."

"I'm tired; I'll talk to you tomorrow." Click.

He called first thing the next morning. In a stern voice, "What are you doing?"

"I'm getting ready for work."

"I've thought about it, and we'll go on with our plans, but I want you to know, I'm not thrilled."

"Sweetie, I don't want to be married to someone who does not want to be married to me. I am getting ready for work and we will talk about this later. Have a great day, I love you, bye."

Chapter 29

The salon was beginning to look like a salon. At first, Zach was enthusiastic about doing the work but not long after he began, he seemed to tire of it. Wayne and all of the other volunteers disappeared as soon as he returned. There was not much work left to do, but he finished it the night before we opened and headed back to Wisconsin.

Desiree decided not to bring the wedding up. She would wait and let him do it. The salon opened in June and Zach was busy building another cottage for Erik. Little did she know he would be purchasing those as well. They were both busy and did mention their plans.

Zach came to town and Desiree had planned for them to go to a festival at the park near her house. They were meeting her friends. They joined everyone in the beer garden. They began congratulating him on their engagement. They raised their glasses, toasted them, Zach smiled, and lifted his glass as though he was as happy as a lark.

Tammy said, "Hey Des, let me see your ring."

"I'm not wearing it."

Zach looked as surprised as everyone else did that she was not wearing it. Evidently, he had not noticed she had taken it off.

The ring was a little too big, but that was not reason Desiree was not wearing it. It no longer felt right to her. Neither of them mentioned it; they just let it go.

Desiree hired a few girls and was optimistic about the future. Zach's cottages were renting, overall, everything was going as planned;

well almost everything. July 4th was approaching and as always, she planned to be with Zach in Wisconsin for the fireworks.

Jake was going to his dad's, and Desiree made up her mind she would talk to Zach about them. She drove up and Zach seemed excited that she was there.

He had made all of the arrangements for them to go to Benny and Mae's but this time he wanted them to go alone on his boat for the fireworks. It might have had something to do with Cheryl being there this year. She had been there the year before when he came with Brenda and now Desiree was going to be there.

The first night she was there, Zach wanted to have a fire. He joined her on the log swing as he held her hand. They were quiet, just gazing into the fire. Desiree spoke first and calmly, "What do you want me to tell everyone about us getting married?"

"I don't give a shit what you tell them."

It was silent for a moment and she asked,

"What should I say to Jake?"

"Just tell him it has been postponed."

"No Zach, I won't do that." He remained quiet the rest of the evening. He had finally given her his answer.

Desiree went in to take a shower and get ready for bed. When opened the cabinet, looking for Q-tips she noticed a bottle of eye crème.

"Zach, whose eye crème is this?" He came in and said,

"It's mine." She examined it a little closer and sure enough, it was men's eye crème. He had never worn eye crème before.

"Since when did you start wearing eye crème? You must have really wanted to impress Julianna."

"You are crazy."

A discussion would be futile; Desiree finished primping and went to bed.

The next night they went to Benny and Mae's cottage. Their daughter introduced Desiree to Cheryl and her husband. Remembering what she had said, she bit her tongue and was cordial. Cheryl was polite but left immediately to go back in the house, without making conversation. Benny and Zach went in to get drinks, leaving Mae and Desiree alone on the deck.

"It is great to see you, Des. Zach told me he could not let you go."

"Well, Mae this is probably the last time I'll be up here. Zach has changed his mind about getting married already and I can't do this anymore."

"He loves you, he told me he did." The guys came out and everyone headed down to the pontoon. They came over on Zach's boat and it was tied to the dock. He and Desiree hopped in and headed toward the middle of the lake. As usual Zach was equipped with whatever would make her most comfortable. He put the top on the boat because it looked like rain. He had extra warm clothes for her, including the hunter's camo jumpsuit he had given Desiree for her birthday the year before. It was the strangest gift she had ever been given. He told her at the time, she was nothing but a f..... spoiled brat.

It sure came in handy that night. Maybe she was a spoiled brat. They had a wonderful evening despite the horrible weather. Another year and another spectacular fireworks display. They waved goodbye and made their way over to the Marina to grab something to eat before going home. They sat down at a table for two in Barn's Marina. A young voluptuous blonde, about 20 years old kept looking over. Finally, she yelled, "Hey, Zachker." He did not seem to hear her. She kept calling him.

"Zach, someone is calling you." He turned his head slowly toward her and without an expression said "hello" and then turned back. He did not attempt to go over there nor did he tell Desiree who she was.

Over all, it was a nice evening and they went home, straight to bed and almost straight to sleep.

Desiree awoke to the smell and sound of sizzling bacon. Zach was always the greatest host, making her feel like she was special all weekend long.

After Desiree washed the dishes and took her shower, Zach was ready to go out on the boat. He had packed the cooler, hooked it to the truck, and rushed Desi out the door. It was a beautiful, warm sunny day. Desiree parked her car at the cottages, so she could just leave from there for home.

As they were driving along the windy, tree-lined road that leads to the Marina, she knew she was not coming back. It seemed that one sad song after another came on the radio. Desiree began to weep as quietly as she could. Zach reached his hand to hers, without a word, and held it all the way there. He seemed to sense what she was thinking, as he was always able to do.

He made it a special day. They fished and he stayed close by, gently kissing her often for no reason at all. They had lunch on the deck at the Marina and back on the boat, they fished.

In the late afternoon, they put away their fishing poles and slowly made their way around the lake. He was pointing out properties he liked and the ones he "almost bought." "Sweetie we may have to stop in and use the restroom soon." she said.

Zach glanced over at the Marina and then at Desiree,

"We are close by, let's go now."

"I don't have to go right now but I will soon."

He headed for the Marina as if he did not hear her. Desiree felt that once again he was only trying to accommodate her; 'what a sweetheart,' she thought.

As they were nearing his boat slip, she noticed two women on a pontoon; one was squinting against the sun, looking their way. It appeared that she knew Zach and Desiree expected that he would probably introduce them when they arrived. He did not seem to notice her, as he was busy maneuvering the boat in and tying it off. He stayed behind as she shuffled off inside to freshen up.

As she was making her way back outside Desiree noticed, through the window, Zach was on the blonde woman's peer heading back toward the deck. She came out on to the deck and by this time, he was passing the pontoon. The look on the faces of those women was the look of someone who had just witnessed a bad accident. They were staring at him with their mouths wide open. They had an 'I can't believe he is that bold' look on their face. Desiree walked toward him, "What are you doing?"

"I'm just checking the water."

He continued off the peer, passing her as she continued on to the peer. Desiree could not pinpoint the feeling she had but it was a familiar one. He turned and realized she was not following him, and by this time, she was at the end of the woman's peer. The two women seemed frozen with the same look on their faces. Reminding her of the childhood game, she once played. She looked down into the water,

"Yep, that's water." and turned to go back to the boat.

"Sweetie what are you doing?"

"Just checking the water, she sarcastically replied."

The woman was blonde, in her late forties or early fifties. She was on the chunky side but not too heavy. She reeked of money; she was wearing Docker shorts and a golf shirt. Desiree glanced over as she passed them and looking directly at her, greeted her with a smile and said, "Hello."

The look on her face never changed and she did not respond. The men they were with came out and off they went. She seemed to be avoiding looking their way as they disappeared on the lake.

They went back out to finish their tour of the lake. Zach was suddenly talking a mile a minute. It was as though he had filled up on caffeine while she was in the restroom. He looked over at her and stopped in mid sentence. Desiree now had the same expression those women had, wondering what had just taken place. It was nothing she could put her finger on but it was palpable.

"Boy, sweetie you sure got quiet all of a sudden, hey... I love you." Not knowing how to respond and staring off into the distance, she quietly replied,

"I sure did, didn't I?"

The name Julianna ran across her mind. It was getting late, and he insisted they have dinner on the deck before she left. As they were eating

Desiree took a good look around, soaking it all in. Her days had been numbered for a long time. He was making it very difficult for her to be done.

He kissed her goodbye and she was gone. Desiree drove back down the windy road and did not look back. She just wanted to go home.

She had not realized the speed limit had dropped and when she looked in her rear view mirror, she saw the flashing lights. Desiree pulled over.

"Where are you going?"

"Home, to Indiana."

"Where have you been?"

"Wilmington, to see the fireworks."

"Were they good?"

"No, it rained, the weather was terrible."

"Do you know how fast you were going?" the officer asked.

"No."

"75 miles an hour. The speed limit is reduced in this area, because of the lights. Slow down, okay, and have a safe trip home."

"Thank you, I will."

She called Zach, he did not answer.

He called several times later that night and she could not pick up the phone. She knew if she spoke to him, she would not end it, and it needed to be over.

A few days later, he called and said he was coming to pick up his clothes. Desiree cried.

Zach came and they talked. Desiree asked him if he would tell Jake, as she did not have the heart to do it. "

By the way Zach, the woman on the pontoon the last time we went out on your boat, was that Julianna?"

He gently and simply said,

180

"No, sweetie."

"Who was she?"

"You are going to drive yourself crazy."

The next evening he came over for dinner. Jake was helping Desiree in the kitchen and Zach emphatically told him,

"Your mom and I will not be getting married; we have decided to be friends and see where it goes."

Jake's disappointment was obvious, but Desi was not certain whom he felt most sorry for, himself or his mom.

They made small talk during dinner, and Desiree knew Jake was disappointed but Zach would still be around. She wanted Jake to have what he had always dreamed of, a family. He was quiet but seemed okay with it.

Their break-ups never lasted long and before they knew it, Desiree and Zach were back together.

Zach and Desiree went shopping for his mother, and when they went to the checkout, he said to the woman, "Don't forget the lamp." He had purchased the Tiffany lamp Desiree had been admiring and they went home. Zach was living with them again.

Desiree sent her dress back and postponed her trip to Florida. They had a year to use their flights, and the woman at the resort said they would not lose their deposit if they came within the next year.

Desiree had always been an independent girl, and did not have to be married, but for some reason she felt, she would feel more secure if they were married. It had been seven years, and she never dreamed she would stay with someone that long without marrying him. "I have a lot to do. We cannot do anything until Jake leaves for college." It was the summer of 2006. Zach's reasoning did have some validity so she accepted his explanation and they went on the way it was.

Another weekend at the lake, boating, fishing, and relaxing with a good book was just what the doctor ordered. Zach always made certain that she felt pampered when they were away, something she found difficult to get use to.

He needed to clean the cottages and get them ready for the next tenants. It was an unusually hot day and although the nights on the lake were cool, it was uncomfortably warm. She was more than happy to help. They went in the first cottage and while she was dusting and vacuuming Zach was busy filling the sink to wipe the counters, stove, and refrigerator.

"This hot water heater is a good one, the water is still warm."

Thinking nothing of it, she continued vacuuming, singing as she went along. As Zach finished in the kitchen and headed to the bathroom to clean it, she walked over to wipe off the old register in the living room.

"Owe! Zach, come here."

"Sweetie what's wrong" as he rushed in the room.

"The heat is on in here."

He calmly walked over, shut it off, and headed back in to the other room.

"Wait a minute, why is that on? You always turn everything off between rentals, no one rented here last night, and it is ninety degrees today."

"I must have forgotten to turn off the hot water heater too." Seemingly unconcerned, he kept walking,

"Maybe one of the girls from the marina came in here to borrow something."

"What would they want in here?"

"I don't know, maybe they needed the vacuum cleaner."

"You really need to start locking these doors."

"I never lock the doors, this is Wisconsin," he yelled from the bathroom.

"Someone must have spent the night here last night, because it is too hot to have the heat on during the day."

"Baby, I'll be right back, the other cottages are clean but I want to make sure there is plenty of paper towels and toilet paper in them."

He hurried off as she was putting the vacuum cleaner away. She found him in the one bedroom cottage. It was not rented often, as it was small and needed some work. He was in the bathroom emptying the trash.

"Who was in here?"

"Oh, Erik let his cousin stay here last night. He and his girlfriend were too drunk to drive." He seemed angry,

"I am going to have a talk with Erik. They need to at least clean up afterwards." "Strange things happen around here."

Desiree just walked out shaking her head.

Chapter 30

Despite her disappointment, the summer seemed to go by quickly. Desiree was busy working and continuing to add the final touches to the salon. They were heading into her favorite season; Fall. That is why she had chosen September to be married and the date was quickly approaching. It did not dawn on her that Zach had remembered the date until it had come and gone.

On that morning in September, he mentioned he was going to go by Al's place to visit him for a while. Desiree decided it would be as good a time as any to clean the garage. It was long past due and, besides it would keep her busy for a better part of the day.

She did not pay attention to how much time had passed and began to wonder why Zach had not returned. As she continued, Desiree realized he knew what day it was and was avoiding her.

Desiree became angrier as time went on. Here she was cleaning the garage on her wedding day. 'Not only should he be doing this, after all he is living here rent-free, it is my wedding day for God's sake!' She went inside and called him.

"Where are you?"

By the time he rolled in the driveway, Desiree was furious. He walked in the garage as she was sweeping. It had been five hours and she was finishing up. She did not look up or acknowledge him, she just continued sweeping in a manner as if it were his head lying there.

"What's wrong?" he asked.

"You opened that can of worms," as she stopped dead in her tracks, "we were supposed to get married today, and you just disappear for five hours, while I spend it cleaning the garage! The least you could have done was to ask me out for dinner, but instead you humiliate me more, by leaving me for five hours; how dare you!"

"Give me that broom, I'll finish."

"I am finished, no thanks." He grabbed the broom, and swept up the debris without another word. The rest of the day was uneventful and frankly, she was impressed he even remembered the date. She was even more impressed that she stood up to him.

On Sunday evening, the last week of September, she had all but forgotten about that day, and was busy in the kitchen, peeling potatoes for dinner.

Zach's cell phone rang and when he answered it, he made his way outside. 'How many times had this happened?' she thought. 'Does he not realize how obvious this is?'

He came in, and came up behind Desiree, slid his arms around her waist and nuzzled her neck and began licking her ear. For the first time, she was not in the mood.

"Hey baby, are you coming up North this weekend?"

Desiree whirled around; this scenario was becoming all too familiar.

"What is going on? Zach."

"I just need to know if you are coming up this weekend."

"I thought that was the plan, we've already talked about it."

"Okay, I just wanted to know so I could make plans if you weren't coming."

He set the table while she was getting dinner ready. Jake came downstairs and they all sat down together to eat. This was Jake's favorite time, everyone sitting together at the dinner table, having someone to pass the food to and, making conversation. He loved that.

"Hey," Zach asked,

"Is it October 1ˢᵗ this weekend, because if it is, you know what I'll be doing. It's hunting season."

Desiree looked at him and smiled. 'Nice try,' she thought. 'I am going to Wisconsin for sure now.' Before Jake excused himself from the table, he asked if Jake was going up with him fishing the following weekend. They had made those plans as well.

"You need to let me know, and you have about five minutes to decide." She thought he must have been kidding; it was difficult to tell sometimes.

"Sure, I'll go." He excused himself and went to do his homework, while he watched ESPN. She did not have a clue how he maintained his 4.0 status, but she certainly could not complain. Jake was such a good boy. She would just sit and cry sometimes, wondering what she ever did to deserve such wonderful children.

When Zach went up to bed, he wanted Desiree to go too. They went around 10 o'clock as usual and once again, she was having trouble falling asleep.

About 1 am, Zach's cell phone rang. Desiree jumped up and, ran downstairs to answer it, but by the time she got down there, it had stopped ringing.

Barely awake he came running down the stairs,

"What's going on?"

"It's after 1 o'clock in the morning, and your cell phone is ringing, you tell me."

He picked it up to listen to the message, and when the volume went up, she relaxed when she heard a man's voice but could not make out what he was saying. As he hung up the phone, Zach said,

"Can you believe a salesman is calling me this late about a part for a furnace for the crematory I am building? He must be from the east coast."

With that, he went upstairs and went right back to sleep. She looked at caller id on his phone; it was a Wisconsin area code, which indicated the call was coming from Grand Waters, Wisconsin; an hour from his cabin. At least one of them could sleep.

The next morning at breakfast Desiree asked,

"If the guy who called during the night was on the east coast, wouldn't it have been even later for him?"

"I meant to say he must be calling from the west coast."

Desiree dropped it once again. Every time she felt she was getting close to catching him, something else would happen to take her in another direction. If she could catch him red-handed then she could walk away. She really needed to learn to trust him, and as he would always remind her,

"You think too much."

He was not the first person to say that, so maybe he was right. She needed to work on that.

On Friday, Desiree made the long drive to Wisconsin, noticing Zach was not calling along the way, as he usually did.

She called him to let him know where she was. He was not in his usual good mood.

When she finally arrived, there was no greeting; he was sitting on the sofa. He mentioned he had made brownies. He made them in his toaster oven, as he did not have a stove in the cabin; he never ceased to amaze her.

"Where would you like to go for dinner?" he asked.

"Let's go to Applebee's."

"I heard about this place in Fountain View, let's go there."

'Why did he bother to ask?'

Fountain View was a small town out in the middle of nowhere, as was Fremont, the town Zach lived in. Desiree agreed to go there, wondering why he never wanted to go to Wilmington. It was the largest town near him and he mentioned going there often when she was not with him.

There was Mitchell's, Sport's Pub, The Beach Club, and Jimmy's Brewery that Brenda's friend owned. She had never been to any of these places and had suggested them many times.

They went in, seated themselves, and as she looked around, wondered who had told him about this place. It was not clean and sparsely decorated. The food was no better and as this crossed her mind, he asked,

"Do you like this place?"

'He must be kidding,' she thought. Finally, she was beginning to verbalize what she was thinking.

"No, I don't. It is dirty, and the food is terrible. Why don't you ever take me to Wilmington, I've never been to Mitchell's."

"Oh, after Labor Day the tourists leave and they're trying to get rid of leftover food."

'You are kidding me! Do I have stupid written across my forehead,' and as that was the look she shot back as well; he changed the subject.

The next morning, there was no smell of bacon sizzling on the portable burners. She dragged herself out of bed, only to find Zach in his usual position, looking out the window waiting for the next bird or animal to come meandering by.

"Good morning sweetheart."

"Good morning Sweetie, did you sleep well?"

"Yep I did, how about you?"

"Good, let's go back to bed, I'll race ya," and they ran back to his room, and jumped in bed. They laid there for about five minutes when suddenly he sprang from the bed and left the room.

As he was pulling his jeans up, he said,

"I forgot to go to the cottages and collect the rent!"

"Zach, strange things happens around you." His head spun around to look at her as though she had caught him doing something. How many times had she relived this moment? Desi remembered one time during one of his business deals when Zack hung up the phone only to say,

"It's time for head games."

"Zach, you are a master manipulator." There were the many times he told her, "I am a simple and, private guy." "Zach there is a difference in being private and being secretive." He would spin his head around to look at her and then go on as if nothing had happened.

He ran into the bathroom to brush his teeth and Desiree decided to get up and go into the living room. There was not enough time for her to get ready to go with him but he said he would not be gone long, and out the door, he went.

It was difficult getting used to his constant change in plans and sudden decisions, but that is just who he was and she accepted that. At least she thought she had. Anytime he left Desiree alone, her mind would go in to PI mode.

She went into his office to see if the computer was connected. She walked in and saw the computer lying on Jake's bunk beds that were in his office.

As she turned to walk out, she could not help but notice an Applebee's receipt lying there. She picked it up; it had yellowed from age and seemed out of place lying on his current mail. She looked at the date, 12/04/2005.

It was almost a year old, so why was it lying here? She looked at the rest of it and noticed two guests were served. The order included veggie pizza, Kailua, and cream. Scotch and soda was on the list as well. Desi knew Zach had been there with someone, so yet another direction to go in. 'He would not take me to Applebee's last night and here is a receipt from there, where apparently he had taken someone else a long time ago.'

He had been dating Julianna around that time. In addition, Brenda's birthday was around December 1, which she had found out during her 'investigation' that he had taken her there before. Desiree thought back to the year before last and it was around then, she had asked him about using his Applebee's card, Joe had given him. That was confirmed when she looked at his credit card statement, only to find his gift card was not enough to cover the bill, and he was charged an additional $35.00 in November, 2004. She felt it was obvious he had left this one for Desiree to find. But, why? She was indeed driving herself crazy.

He came in and said the renters were still fishing and he could not find them to get the rent, so they would have to go back later.

He asked, "Is there something wrong?"

"No, she replied, I just want to get out of here."

"Let's go to town and look around."

"I don't care where we go as long as we get out of here." She took her shower and was ready to go.

Zach seemed to be in a better mood and the day was surprisingly fun. They went to a few stores and he announced he was hungry. They passed Mitchell's Restaurant.

"Oh that is where Mitchell's is."

"Do you want to go there for lunch?" he asked as they passed by. Feeling somewhat confused, She bit her tongue remembering how "bad the food was after Labor Day." 'Had he not told me that just last night?'

Zach and Desiree stopped at a little café and had breakfast. They decided they would go to the cottages, collect the rent, go fishing, and then take the boat over to see Benny and Mae, at their place. As always, Benny and Mae were a hoot.

On Sunday, Zach and Desi went back to Indiana and back to work. The strange calls continued and, try as she might they upset her every time. Desiree could not understand for the life of her why he could not speak on the phone in front of her if the calls were innocent.

Zach was good looking but every woman in Indiana, Wisconsin and the surrounding states could not want him. She could not help but feel there was something wrong with her. She decided to go see someone.

Desiree had been to see a psychiatrist once. She felt as if she was jumping out of her skin all of the time. The doctor had prescribed Zoloft. After her first visit, she decided this was going to be too expensive and settled for a psychologist. Zach told Desiree he was so proud of her for getting help, and was sure it would be good for her. Her head was spinning, and she was constantly confused. Desiree longed for the days when, while her life was not perfect, at least she was in control of it. How and when this happened she could not now remember.

She confided in a few friends about what she was doing, only to get the same response from all of them.

"There is nothing wrong with you; Zach has the problem, not you."

When she told her friend Theresa, she responded in the same manner and added "Before Zach, did you ever have three drinks and then black out? Did you ever go to a psychologist? Did you ever take anti-depressants or anti-anxiety medication? Think about this Desiree. It is not you, it's him."

She continued to go a few more times. She asked Zach,

"Will you go with me for moral support?"

"Sure, baby." He went for the following visit and Desiree was surprised when the Psychologist's focus was on him for the entire hour she had paid for. They shook hands then sat down. She looked at Zach and said,

"Desiree is having some difficulty with understanding what is going on in your relationship. She is confused and would like to know where this is going, and what your intentions are."

"Well, I have told her, when her son leaves for college, we will be together."

"What exactly does be together mean to you, Zach? Does it mean married?"

He did not hesitate. "Yes."

"Yes, you will legally marry Desiree when Jake leaves for college."

"Yes."

"That is several years down the road, isn't it?"

"Yes."

"You know that you want to be married to Desiree then, is that right?"

"Yes."

"Well Zach, tell me something, if you know that you want to be married to Desiree several years down the road, why don't you just marry her, now?"

"I have a lot to do. I'm trying to retire early, and it's just is not the right time." At the end of the session, she asked if he would consider coming in for his own counseling.

"If we can negotiate your rate, I will consider it." He refused to go back; he always had something else to do.

She went back to her a few more times, relaying some of the bizarre things that were happening. She said,

"He could be doing anything as far as you know." She assured Desiree there was nothing wrong with her and encouraged her to continue working on herself. She could not fix Zach; he would have to do that himself. Desiree stopped taking the Zoloft. She did not feel right on it and it felt as if she was just masking the issue. She wanted to deal with it straight on.

Chapter 31

When they were slow at the salon, the girls would use the Internet. It was useful when they needed to research products and order items for the salon, but they began using it to get on 'My Space'.

Desiree had heard of My Space but had never been on it. It was fairly new and she had only recently begun to surf the net. Karen seemed to be the biggest offender. Instead of doing what needed done, she was online chatting with friends from other states, as well as her hometown in New York.

While surfing one day she asked,

"What did you say Brenda from Wisconsin's last name was?"

"Stiller," she replied.

In less than a minute she said, "Oh here she is."

"What do you mean?"

"She's on My Space and she's not all that good looking." Desiree walked over and there she was, kissing a young army man. Desiree assumed he was her son.

She was not beautiful but Desiree thought she was rather attractive. Her hair was fine shoulder length like hers, and highlighted like hers as well. She looked to be almost as tall as her son was, and of average size; they could have passed for relatives.

"Where is the 5'2", 150 pounds, and gray hair?" Desiree caught herself asking aloud.

She watched in amazement as Karen showed her this website, and although Desi knew it had been created for entertainment, she could see where, in the wrong hands, this sight could be used for many negative things.

She became curious and found herself online. She began entering names she knew, just to see if any of them were on My Space and was surprised to find that some were.

Just for kicks, she put in the name Zach and his zip code, not for one second thinking it would pop up. Not only did Zach not have the Internet, how many Zach's could live in Fremont, population zero.

To her horror, it came up. It looked to be a site where he had put in the wrong information, and as little as possible, so he could cruise the site. She had noticed many people do that. The date last used was November 2004.

It took a few days for this to sink in. Desiree thought back to that time, and it was around then Zach's phone would go straight to voicemail or he would not answer it.

She remembered that was also around the time she called him back, only to hear him say, "Hey, what's going on?" when he thought she was someone else. He did not say who he thought she was, but had apologized for days afterward.

It would also answer the question about having someone else's phone line running in his gray box. During her investigating, Desiree had found the name of the guy who owned that number.

While playing around on the computer one night, she decided to check her neighborhood for registered sex offenders. She then entered Jason's address to make sure there were none living near her grandchildren. Just for the heck of it, she entered Zach's as well.

Desiree was horrified to find that the guy, who had his phone line running into Zach's box, was indeed a registered sex offender. All those times she had spent on his eighty acres, where it was pitch dark at night while he was at work, made the hair on the back of her neck stand up. Pieces of the puzzle were beginning to fit. That explained the extra phone line. It would also explain, why in the dead of winter, he was running an extra line into his office,

"Just in case I ever get the Internet."

Was he on the porn site at her house, like the woman at Phone Company tried to tell her?

Zach came home that night and she said,

"I have something to show you."

"What is it?"

"A picture of Brenda. She's on My Space." He took the paper from her hand and stared at it for what seemed like forever.

"It looks like her," he said as he handed it back.

"It looks like her because it is her."

"So what," he replied in an annoyed voice.

"Show me 5'2", 150 pounds, and gray hair Zach."

"She does have gray hair. I am not a good judge of height and weight, but she is definitely not thin. Where did you get this?" He was visibly angry.

"On the Internet. What difference does it make?"

His impatience and anger was quite evident. Desiree had not seen him this angry since the time she asked him about the second number in his gray box.

"You need to stop investigating me, and stay out of my business."

"As long as you and I have been together we should not have separate business, Zach. Your business is my business, and my business is your business." Once again, the next morning, Zach disappeared without a word; he just simply vanished.

Desiree passed him on Route 41 coming from the direction of Cedar Lake.

He was so secretive, repeatedly saying opposite things. When she questioned this, he would calmly say,

"I never said that." She could not let go of some of the remarks he had made.

Thinking back on the evening when they were sitting on the veranda at Al's place, and Zach mentioned that Desiree had called him while he was sitting in a tree stand waiting to catch a beaver.

They were destroying the trees on his property. With a smirk on Al's face,

"Let me get this straight, you were hunting beaver when the beaver called?"

Zach, looking expressionless at Al, and replied with a straight face,

"You can't get enough of those." Al grinned like a Cheshire cat. He was looking directly at Zach as though they were sending each other telepathic messages. Zach walked away and Al said to her,

"Boy he has a way with words doesn't he?" Zach had always accused Desiree of living under a rock. Apparently, he believed his accusation.

Desiree later mentioned this to Zach and he said,

"You must have misunderstood."

Her head seemed to be swimming constantly as though she had been sucked into the eye of a tornado, and the force was so great, it held her there. She tried to end their relationship again. Only when he was gone did she calm down, but she desperately missed him. She loved him and could not see the vicious cycle she was living in. It was reminiscent of a child who attempted to walk after being spun too quickly on a merry-go-round.

Desiree would come into work only to hear that Zach was driving up and down the side road that leads to a large apartment complex behind her salon. There was a large window in the salon that faced the side street. He would stop to look in, until someone saw him, and then would slowly proceed to the intersection. Desiree interpreted his behavior with, 'He misses me.'

He never seemed embarrassed by this, and did not seem to care who saw him either. That was another reason she thought, 'he must love me a lot to make such a fool of himself.'

One evening she was talking to the girls. It was nearing closing time and she was more than ready to go home. Desiree stepped to the door and when she finally focused on the big, white truck she was staring passed, she recognized it.

Desiree was thinking about the time when Zach said,

"Hey wouldn't you love to wake in the morning and have me roll over and ask what are we doing today? That is going to happen, if you will just be patient. We can spend the summers in Wisconsin and take care of the cottages, keep your place in Indiana, and spend the harshest months in Florida."

That sure sounded good to her right now. She was getting tired. The phone ringing jolted Desiree back to reality and she grabbed it.

"Hello."

"Hey, what is going on?"

"Nothing, Zach."

"I owe you an apology."

"For what?"

"I was coming from the Quest, I needed cigarettes, and when I saw you standing in the door I was too embarrassed to stop in." There was a Smoke Shop next to her salon, but there were many in the area, including right next to the Quest.

He seemed to be slurring his words and the more he spoke, the more obvious it was that he was drunk.

"Where are you?"

"Sitting in my truck."

"Are you driving?"

"No, I'm sitting Mom's driveway."

"Why are you sitting in the driveway?"

"Trish is here visiting, and I just wanted to apologize, like I said, I only wanted cigarettes."

"Don't worry about it, Zach."

"Its Christmas time and I'd like to take you out for dinner."

"Why don't you go in and visit with Trish, and we'll talk about this tomorrow."

"Okay, but I was just coming for cigarettes."

"I'll talk to you tomorrow, goodnight."

He called the next day, and once again, she made the decision to meet with him, could it hurt? It was a holiday, she missed him, and he obviously felt the same. If only he could get over his fear of commitment.

He came to the salon around closing time and she told him they would take her car, as there was no sense in taking both vehicles. He agreed. Desiree turned off the lights and they went to the parking lot.

"Wait a minute," he said. Zach went to his truck and pulled out a large box wrapped in a black trash bag. He always presented gifts wrapped in newspaper or a bag. He did not believe in wasting money on wrapping paper; only in the beginning when he was trying to impress her, did he swing for gift-wrap.

He had mentioned he wanted to get Jake something for Christmas and Desiree thought nothing of it. They went to Dick's Restaurant and settled in the same booth where he had proposed.

They ordered the usual, but there was no proposal. They had dinner, made small talk, and drove back to the salon, where he had left his truck.

She inquired,

"By the way, how many Zach's live in Fremont?"

"Believe it or not, there are a few, why?"

"Did you know there is a Zach on My Space, who lives in Fremont?"

He laughed,

"No wonder you think something is going on, now I understand why you have been acting crazy lately. Let me see that."

They went in the salon; she entered his name into her computer and showed him.

"Can I have a copy of this? I want to take one up to Dave, and have him investigate who is using my name."

When Desiree was getting ready to leave, he said,

"By the way, that gift is for you."

She went home and had to admit she could not wait to see what it was. She opened it and was pleasantly surprised to find a Kitchen Aid mixer. Desiree baked a lot and this gift was thoughtful and perfect.

She called to thank him, the conversation was short, they said goodnight. The next day while at work, Jake called.

"Mom, Zach called and asked if he could take me shopping to pick out my Christmas presents."

"What did you tell him?"

"I told him, sure but I thought I'd better call you and ask if it's okay."

"Sure it's okay; make sure you pick something good." They laughed and she went back to work.

Zach asked if she would go out with him again and Desiree agreed. He took her to the Town Club in Highland, one of his mother's favorite restaurants, and Desiree liked it as well.

They had a wonderful time; they always found it easy to talk to each other. That dinner lasted four hours. They discussed trivial things and then talked about their relationship.

"I wish you would just trust me, and we could follow our hearts."

She could not count how many times she had heard that, Desiree changed the subject. He mentioned he would be spending Christmas in Wisconsin.

"Why don't you stay here?" she asked.

He responded,

"I have things to do."

She let it go; thinking he probably had made other plans.

He left for Wisconsin and Desi could not help but wish he had stayed. He called constantly, and she texted him to tell him he should have just stayed here.

He texted back, saying,

"I was not invited by anyone I wanted to spend time with."

Desiree was furious and fired off another text.

"I thought maybe you were sniffing up someone else's skirt up there, again!"

He called her and said,

"This is ridiculous. I had a long conversation with my mom, she says there has to be something between us to last eight years, and we need to work it out. I love you."

"I love you too, Zach, and this is ridiculous, you're spending Christmas alone up there, while I'm spending Christmas alone down here."

With that he replied,

"I'm coming home tomorrow, we're going to fix this, and whatever it takes we're going to be together."

Chapter 32

The holidays of 2006 were over and Zach was back to his double life. He was living with them once again. On the weekends, he would often go to Al's to visit. It was late morning on Sunday and he said he was going to go over to see Al. It was Desi's day off and although she felt he should spend time with her, she did not say a word. About an hour after he left, Desiree decided to go for a ride. She headed toward Lynwood. Why, she did not know, but she had always thought he spent a lot of time there. It was the next town over from Highland but across the state line. As she was about to pass the street Al lived on, she called Zach.

"Hi babe, where are you at?"

"I am sitting in Al's driveway waiting for him to come home so we can go have a beer."

Desiree could see Zach's truck sitting in the driveway as she passed by. Zach was not in it. "Why, where are you?"

"I'm just going for a drive, I'll see you later." That was strange; what is he up to now? Desiree was growing tired of trying to catch him in the act just so she could leave the relationship.

"You think too much, just trust me," he would always remind her. However, she did not and he was either brilliant in his deceit or she was crazy. Desiree was beginning to believe it was a little of both. He was way too smart for this naïve, gullible girl. She drove home.

Desiree lost two more brothers: John had passed away in August 2006 at the age of 64, while Will died aged 63 in February 2007. Her family had gone through enough tragedy when in March they had also lost their nephew, Trevor, Raquel's middle son, at the young age of 26. Desiree's life seemed to be spiraling out of control and she longed for stability now more than ever.

Zach was using her computer to look for a truck to buy and noticed that Julianna's name was in her search history; he vanished once again.

After looking up Julianna's name on the computer, Desiree had found Julianna had over 40 different addresses. She then looked up the name Gayla Burnhart and she was listed at over 40 addresses as well. Some of the addresses were from towns around her area in Indiana. The majority for Gayla's however, were in Wilmington and the surrounding area, while the majority of the listings for Julianna were in Reno and Las Vegas. This was odd. Brenda also had addresses near her, but most were listed in Wisconsin. Sometime earlier, Gayla's name had been on Zach's caller id. She did not know who she was but she knew that Zach did. She asked him one night,

"Sweetie do you know a Gayla Burnhart?"

With agitation in his voice,

"What, are you writing a book? How do you know her?"

"I know she used to live in Hobart and Chesterton and now lives in Wilmington. I just wondered if you knew her."

"Nope." Desiree had more questions than answers and one led to another. This reminded her of another girl named Karen Getzlaff, whose phone number was also on his phone.

They went out for dinner and Zach told Desiree once again, in a calm but more desperate voice, to stay out of his business.

"I am almost where I want to be, if you can just hold on a little longer. I want to have a million dollars and I am almost there." She was staring at him searching for deception in his eyes, his voice, and his body language. There was nothing but calmness. Sometimes she felt he was too calm, seemingly void of emotion. His answer to that would always be, "You are too emotional and I use common sense." He was right; 'I do allow my emotions to rule at times.'

"Sometimes I get the overwhelming feeling of being caught naked in a snowstorm," she continued.

"There you go again, you worry too much." He demonstrated with a quarter, moving it along the tabletop.

"I am heading in a straight line toward my dream."

He began to move the quarter back and forth across the table, representing Desiree.

"You keep telling me, it has been three years, it has been four years, it has been five years, and who gives a shit." He then began moving it in a straight line.

"Meanwhile I am heading straight toward my goal and I need you to roll with me. No one or nothing is going to keep me from reaching my goal."

"Are you doing this for us?"

"I am doing this for me right now."

"Zach, would you like to know what I found when I looked Julianna up on the computer?"

"What?"

"She has over 40 addresses in Reno and Las Vegas. What did she do for a living? Was she a hooker? Is that why you were adamant about not wanting me to know what she did for a living?"

Evidently, he felt it was better for her to know the truth than to go on believing that, so finally after all this time, he answered her question.

"She bought, remodeled, and sold houses."

She began to absorb his answer when a light came on, another piece to the puzzle. There had been one woman after another, all seemingly in the same business. Were all of these women somehow involved in real estate? Gayla had over 40 addresses as well and, apparently, she was in the same line of work. Could that be a coincidence?

"I see, you thought you found your meal ticket, didn't you. Were you looking to date a woman with money who could give you endless jobs? Remember telling me you were tired of chasing."

"No babe. I want to be with you, otherwise why would I be here?"

Desiree tried to keep it where it was, in the past.

They continued to see each other but he was living at his mother's house. They spoke every day. He was always telling her how much he was doing for her and how much his mother appreciated it. Desi got the feeling he was manipulating her and trying to get her to let him move back in; after all, she could use some help too. It was not going to work this time.

Around the end of March 2007, Zach came by the salon to see her. He refused to go get lunch for her. He had never refused before and Desiree did not know what she had done this time. She guessed since she would not allow him to live with her, this was her punishment.

Zach called that night to say he had gone to a bar with Al and he just did not believe she could handle him going back and forth to Wisconsin.

"Wait a minute Zach, why do you feel that after commuting for four years that suddenly I cannot handle it?"

"I just don't think you can." With that, he said good night and hung up the phone.

She did not see or hear from him for nine days. The following weekend Desiree went to the movies with her friend, Lars; he wanted to see 'Wild Hogs.' It was hilarious and she enjoyed it; there was no pressure and afterwards they went their separate ways. While they were there, Zach had called her cell phone and left a message.

"I just wondered if you would like to go see a movie, call me."

She decided to go to Wal-mart to get the ingredients for cookies. As she was crossing the parking lot, Zach pulled up. Desiree's first thought was, 'he must have installed a GPS tracker on my car, as he seems to know where I am all of the time.'

"I'm here to price a filter for my truck." His truck was new and she doubted it needed a filter.

"Would you like to go to the movies?"

"I just came from the movies Zach but I'll go again; you know I love the movies."

He never explained where he had been for nine days and she never asked. It did not really matter much to her anymore. Desiree was still in love with Zach but was tired of trying to stop a 'runaway train.'

When her nephew Trevor passed away as always Zach was there. This time though there were others there to help and he seemed to feel threatened by it.

She could not shake the deep feeling within her as hard as she tried. The thought that Zach had a personality disorder kept running through her mind. She kept trying to prove she was wrong and the more she tried, the more she began to realize maybe she was not the crazy one after all.

Chapter 33

Her vacation was coming up at the end of April and Desiree could not wait to leave. With all the deaths in her family and dealing with Zach, she felt upside down. At first, Zach was upset that she was using their reservations to go, but he relented and said to go ahead. He also called her to let her know someone had invited him to go to Florida. She suspected that that someone was Brenda; but she did not ask.

The morning came for Desiree to leave and the doorbell rang. She thought it was probably her sister, Raquel and her boyfriend coming to pick her up to take her to the airport.

Desiree opened the door and there Zach was with that same smile and an arm full of goodies. He had Fannie May 'turtles', her favorite, purple flowers, her favorite color, and breakfast, which consisted of a McDonald's sausage McMuffin and a coke. He wanted to take her to the airport but she already had a ride. He kissed Desi, told her he loved her, and left.

The weather was gorgeous but she had mixed feelings. Desiree was sad that she was there alone using what should have been her honeymoon reservations. At the same time, she found peace there.

When she arrived, she drove to the resort knowing the first night she would not have a room with a view. Desi loved the water. She cherished the sound of the waves crashing to the shore and just watching the tide roll in. The resort was overbooked and they promised her she could have the spot with the view she wanted the following day. Because there had been a mistake, they had promised a gift certificate to the café in the village. She was just happy to be there.

Zach had begged for the key to her house so he could take care of her cat; and Desiree relented. She began getting text messages almost immediately. He called or texted several times a day.

Her gift certificate came and the property manager made Desiree promise to use it.

"I want you to go down to Blasé and have a good time. They will take good care of you there, they already know that you're coming, so meet people and have some fun." Being alone made it difficult to venture out, but later that week she decided she would do just that.

Desiree showered, dressed, and made her way down to the village. She stopped at the first place she came to, The Beach House. Desiree reluctantly went in and sat at the bar. It was early and there were not many people there. The bartender smiled and said,

"May I help you?"

"May I have a Margarita, please?"

"You sure can."

She savored it, knowing that she could not have many because she was alone. She sipped on it for a long time, listening to the piped music, watching couples laughing, drinking, and enjoying what was probably their vacation too. She decided to take a walk, as the weather was gorgeous. She strolled down the sidewalk, trying to take it all in. She knew from experience how quickly the time goes here and she wanted to enjoy every minute of it.

She reached Café Blasé and remembered being there before. Shelly and Desiree had been there and loved the food. It had typical, tropical décor. It was eclectic with a restaurant and bar inside and a bar on the deck outside. She went in and walked up to the bar, where a smile greeted her. The bartender asked,

"May I get you something?"

"Do you make Mojitos?"

"Sure do, can I make you one?"

"Yep." She handed her the gift certificate, the bartender smiled and handed her a drink.

"Thank you very much." Desiree proceeded out to the deck, as she wanted to sit outside and enjoy the weather. As she sat down, she thought 'it does not get any better than this.'

It did not matter much where she went on the island; everyone was friendly and seemed to be having a good time. Desiree sat down at the bar on the deck looking around, when she sneezed.

As she pulled at the only thing she had at her disposal, the napkin under her glass, out of nowhere a gorgeous man appeared. He was lean, over six feet tall, with jet-black wavy hair, dark brown eyes, and a beautiful smile that seemed to light up; she looked around for the genie that granted this wish.

"Vy ahl you clying? She was not sure where the accent came from but she liked it.

"I'm not crying."

He moved closer,

"Vy ahl you so sad?"

"I'm not sad, I simply sneezed."

He walked away. Desiree noticed he stayed close by and at one point; he stopped and asked,

"Vhat time ahl you leaving?"

"Soon," she replied.

She had forgotten what the property manager had said earlier,

"They know you are coming." This must be what they meant when they added, "Don't worry about a thing, they'll take good care of you, there."

Two girls walked up and sat next to Desi at the bar. They began chatting as they were from out east. They became fast friends, telling each other where they were from and exchanging phone numbers.

Jen leaned over and said,

"I don't know who that guy is, standing behind you, but I would go for that if I were you. He's good looking."

Desiree laughed,

"He is probably my son's age."

Jen asked, "How old are you?"

"I'm 51."

"I hope I look like you when I am 51," she replied.

Desiree thought that was nice, most women do not compliment others; a sure sign she was comfortable in her own skin. She was beginning to feel comfortable as well, and glad she had decided to venture out.

Desiree told the girls to have fun, but she had to go. It was only 9:30 pm but she was alone and did not want to take any chances. Desiree crossed the street and as she rounded the corner; there he was. Oddly enough, she was not afraid and they continued walking toward the resort as if they had planned it this way.

When they reached the beach, they crossed the road and continued walking by the water.

"So, vhat is youl stoly?"

"I just got out of an eight year relationship and I'm here to heal from it."

"I undelstand, I had a five yeal lelationship and it was also bad." He took her hand and pulled her along the shore and they began to run. They were in the water, out of the water, like two kids discovering something for the first time. They finally stopped and he kissed her.

"You have no idea how old I am."

"I do too, but I don't cale how old you ahl. Do you have an ink pen?" Desi pulled one from her purse and handed it to him. He wrote something in the palm of his hand. He would not allow her to look. The night air was warm and intoxicating. There was a gentle breeze sweeping from the Gulf and the stars lit up the sky. They were the only ones on the beach that night.

They began running again, faster this time when her legs became entangled in his and they went tumbling onto the sand. Suddenly he was looking down at her and said,

"I do not need to know youl name and I do not need to know youl numbel. You cannot live heel, and I cannot come thel. Thel is no leason to get oul emotions involved."

She began to realize exactly what was going on. He was offering a one-night stand. He helped her up and hand-in-hand, they walked. Quietly at first and he then began to tell her a little bit about himself.

"I vulked fol Nike and was living in Tennessee. I was involved in a vely bad lelationship and am financially tied up in it. I ended up heel and am vulking at the Café until I figule out vhat I vil do with the lest of my life."

They walked across the street to the resort where Desiree was staying and sat on the porch swing. The property owner and his girlfriend came over with a beer for him.

Desiree went in to use the restroom, leaving the door open, turning on the lights and the stereo as she made her way.

When she came out, he was sitting on the sofa.

"Okay, my name is Lafael, vhat is youl name?"

"Desiree Peters."

"No, vhat is youl leal name?"

"That is my real name."

As he reached for his cell phone, he asked,

"Vhat is youl numbel?" she told him and he entered it in his phone.

He stood up and said; "By the way, I am thilty yeals old. " I vil call you Satulday." and he left. Desiree stood in front of the mirror, wondering 'what in the world are you thinking; you are 51 years old acting as if you are 15.' Her hair was a mess, her jeans felt like concrete, and gravity seemed to be pulling them off. Yes, water and sand do make concrete. Desiree wondered if he had left any boot prints, and she laughed at the thought. She showered, went to bed, and slept like a baby.

Zach continued to text and call. Finally, Desiree returned the call.

"Zach, I came here to relax and to get myself together so I can move on. What do you want from me, do you want to be married to me?"

"Yes, I do" he said matter of factly.

"Are you going to stop hanging out in bars?"

"Yes, I will."

That took her aback and she thought that maybe she should rethink this. Desiree went to bed but did not sleep as well as the previous night. She woke up the following morning, got ready, and walked over to the beach, trying to replay the events of the previous night. It was the last thing she expected to happen and it seemed surreal, like a dream. She went over, grabbed a lounge chair, sat down, and began to write. The day went by quickly and Desiree was feeling hungry. She hopped in her rental car and drove off the island to go to the fish market. They cooked fresh fish for her while she waited and wrapped it up; she paid the clerk and drove back.

It was Thursday night and the only night Zach did not call.

Fresh fish on the beach, she believed she had died and gone to heaven. When she finished her meal and cleaned up, she gave Zach a call.

"Hey what are you doing?"

"I'm having dinner with Tim."

Desiree could hear girls laughing and talking in the background,

"Where are you?"

"At a bar near Lynwood."

"What bar?"

"Just a bar near Lynwood."

Feeling frustrated,

"Zach, what is the name of the bar?"

"Here's to You."

"Why didn't you just say that?"

"I didn't know that you knew of any bars around Lynwood."

"I have heard of that bar, I know exactly where it is." He changed the subject, getting anything out of him was like pulling teeth.

Before she knew it, it was time to go. She was sad to leave but it had been wonderful and she would never forget it. Rafael made Desiree feel desirable again, and some of the self-confidence she once possessed was beginning to come back.

Zach asked if he could pick her up from the airport and of course, she said yes. When she got in the truck, he took Desiree's hand and kissed her.

"Did you miss me?"

"Yes, I missed you."

They went home and he moved in. She wanted so much to believe that he loved her and, that the last eight years was not in vain. It was the end of April 2007. Where had the time gone? Desiree hoped that, this time he was ready to settle down. The first night back, he informed her,

"I'll have to bring my clothes back a little at a time."

"Why?"

"Because, Mom is used to me being there. She'll be upset when I leave again."

"Well I guess that makes sense."

During one of their conversations, Zach had reconsidered; he did not want to be married. She realized, 'He duped me once again,' how stupid she felt, but it did not matter; she really did not even care, anymore.

He was home every night after she got home except for the first two Thursdays and there would not be a third. He had not stopped going to bars as he promised, but as long as he was home at night, it was okay with her.

He had been living with Desiree for two weeks and had not brought any clothes over. She tried to discuss it with him only to have him turn the conversation on her.

"How do I know you did not have sex with someone while you were in Florida?"

"Where did that come from?"

"How do I know?"

"Because I am telling you I didn't."

"If you did I would forgive you."

She was stunned and turned to look directly into his eyes, "Why?"

"Because, I love you and sometimes people slip up."

"Is that what you did, Zach."

The familiar deer in the headlights look again. "I don't know."

"You don't know why you did what you did?"

Still with a fixed stare, "I don't know."

The conversation ended. Once again, Desiree did not know where that question had come from or why he asked.

Zach was leaving the following morning. It was Friday and he was going to Wisconsin for the weekend. He woke up early, said he had to go to Highland and as he had been doing for the past two weeks, he would stop by his mom's, take a shower, brush his teeth and get on the road.

She went to work and around noon, Zach called the salon. Kylie, one of her stylists who inexplicably was not speaking to her said, "Zach wants you to call him as soon as possible, he has a new number."

"Why does he have a new number?" She wondered aloud. Kylie shrugged and handed her the piece of paper where she had written it.

When she was free, Desiree dialed the number, "Why do you have a new number?"

"Oh, I left my phone at your house, so I just swung by Wal-mart and got one of those 'to go' phones." Desiree knew for sure, she was done.

Zach had gone to Highland before he left and had to know he did not have his phone.

It did not ring once the entire weekend; imagine that. It did not matter anymore – it was over for Desiree.

Chapter 34

Thoughts began flooding her mind. A hunter stalks his prey and if he is patient long enough, he will get the prize. After killing a ten pointer and displaying it proudly until the newness wears off, he then wants a twelve pointer to top that, and won't all his buddies be envious? The more ponds he fished in and the more often he fished, if he kept his baited line in long enough, he would catch something. If his catch was small, he just kept throwing it back until he got the big one. If he catches a descent sized one, he may keep it in case he did not get the big one. Something was better than nothing. Desiree supposed she was the descent-sized fish.

Zach was an avid hunter and fisherman and it seemed he was using those same skills to trap, catch, or snare whatever or whomever he set his sights on. He evidently had a bigger fish on the line; and he was becoming reckless in his pursuit. 'Good luck to her.' All of his friends that had money, and whom he felt had looked down on him, would someday be envious. If he went from one attractive woman to another to make money, while they felt trapped in marriages, at last the tables would turn; they would now be jealous of him.

It took Desiree back to a conversation they had long ago.

"Zach, hanging out in bars would be like hunting in an enclosed area of the woods. When you go in, they would hand you a muzzleloader, a bow and arrow, and a shotgun. You could have any deer there and don't worry, if the guy in front of you shoots the one you want, you can just move to the next."

He shook his head,

"You're crazy."

She was really done this time. How often had she said that? It was May 2007, eight years since they began dating.

She was losing her credibility with family and friends. Desiree was growing tired of hearing her own voice in this matter. This had become a vicious cycle. She felt like a puppet on a string, and Desiree now knew whom the puppeteer was. He was about to be one puppet short.

He seemed to have had little sleep when he came home on Sunday. When Desiree came back from a bridal shower, he was fast asleep on her recliner. They did not talk much that evening and went to bed early.

On Monday morning, he woke up early to go to his mother's house to take a shower and run the necessary errands. He was preparing for the biggest job he had ever done. Keith had given him the opportunity to build his building for the trucking company and he wanted to make sure all of his "ducks were in a row."

However, at 9 am he called and asked if she would meet him for breakfast. Desiree agreed. The thoughts of different conversations kept drifting through her mind. She remembered her conversation with Theresa,

"There is nothing wrong with you, it's him." And Dave telling her,

"Des, you have all of the answers." Moreover, Ken told her,

"He's a control freak, it's all about him, and it's all about control."

Time after time, she repeated the same things over, only to have everyone tell her the same thing again and again. It was as though her conscious mind was fighting with her subconscious, and her subconscious was now ready to win.

Zach was sitting there looking at a sales catalog for heavy equipment when Desiree sat across from him. Other than glancing up occasionally, he did not really acknowledge her and continued to browse through the pages.

He glanced up once again

"Something wrong? Did you sleep well last night?"

"Yes I did." He continued to look at the catalog.

"Are you sure you slept well, you seem to be a million miles away, what's wrong?"

"Other than feeling like I am sitting here alone, not much."

"You sure?"

"Zach, I'm upset."

He put the catalog down, "What's up?"

"When I was in Florida, you said you wanted to marry me, until I came home. You said you would be gradually moving your clothes in and you do not even have a pair of socks at my house. You are taking showers and brushing your teeth at your mother's house but you are living and sleeping with me for God's sakes."

"So, what's the big deal?"

"Zach, I want your clothes brought to the house, today, and I want an answer right now."

He sat there staring at her as if she were speaking in another language.

"Zach, I want an answer right now."

The server came and asked if she could get them anything more and then laid down their bill. He stood to get his wallet from his back pocket and without looking at her, he replied flatly,

"I don't have an answer," and with that, he turned and walked away. After eight years, her conscious mind allowed her subconscious to take over.

Chapter 35

Finally, it had become clear to Desiree – this is what he has done his entire life. That is why he cannot stay in one place long. That is why he would abruptly leave and gradually make his way back. He knew she was on the verge of finding out whom and what he was. He would test the waters to see what she knew and when he realized she still had not figured him out, he would come back. He was riding the ride until she would not let him ride anymore.

That is why he begged her to stay out of his business. That is why he said she should not listen to everyone and should just follow their hearts. Desiree had followed her heart and it was leading her straight to Hell. It was all obvious to her now.

During her investigating, Desiree was unable to push back the notion there was something about his personality that just did not feel right. It seemed to her he was two distinctly different people living two distinctly different lives. She finally sat at her computer, went online, and entered personality disorders.

Desiree felt something about him was not right but could never put her finger on what it was. His reaction to things that should have upset him did not, and vice versa. She had convinced herself he was just stronger and more logical than she was.

Being a voracious reader and always 'needing to know everything,' Desiree went online to research personality disorders. As she was searching, she came across narcissism, but when she read further, it said, "Do not rule out the possibility he/she could also be a sociopath. Not all narcissists are sociopaths but all sociopaths are narcissists."

She clicked on the link 'Profile of a Sociopath.' Desiree needed answers so she began to research further.

PROFILE OF A SOCIOPATH

Glibness and Superficial Charm

Manipulative and Conning

They never recognize the rights of others and see their self-serving behaviors as okay. They appear to be charming, yet are covertly hostile and domineering, seeing their victim as merely an instrument. They may dominate and humiliate.

Grandiose Sense of Self

They feel entitled to certain things.

Pathological Lying

They have no problem lying easily and it is almost impossible for them to be truthful on a consistent basis. They can create, and become caught up in, a complex belief about their own abilities. They are extremely convincing and can even pass lie detector tests.

Lack of Remorse, Shame or Guilt

A deep, seated rage, which is split off and repressed, is at their core. They do not see others around them as people, but only as targets and opportunities. Instead of friends, they have victims and accomplices who end up as victims. The end always justifies the means and they let nothing stand in their way.

Shallow Emotions

When they show what seems to be warmth, joy, love, and compassion, it is more feigned than experienced, and serves an ulterior motive. They are outraged by insignificant matters, yet remain unmoved and cold by what would upset a normal person. Since they are not genuine, neither are their promises.

Incapacity for Love

Need for Stimulation

Callousness/Lack of Empathy

They are unable to empathize with the pain of their victims, having only contempt for others' feelings and readily take advantage of them.

Poor Behavioral Controls/Impulsive Nature

Rage and abuse, alternating with small expressions of love and approval produce an addictive cycle for abuser and abused, as well as creating hopelessness in the victim. They believe they are all-powerful, all knowing, entitled to every wish, have no sense of personal boundaries, and no concern for their impact on others.

Early Behavior Problems/Juvenile Delinquency

They usually have a history of academic difficulties, yet "get by" by conning others. They have problems in making and keeping friends.

Irresponsibility/Unreliability

They are not concerned about wrecking others' lives and dreams. They are oblivious or indifferent to the devastation they cause. They do not accept blame, but blame others, even for acts they committed.

Promiscuous Sexual Behavior/Infidelity

Promiscuity and sexual acts of all sorts.

Lack of Realistic Life Plan/Parasitic Lifestyle

They tend to move around a lot or make all encompassing promises for the future, have a poor work ethic but can effectively exploit others.

Criminal or Entrepreneurial Versatility

They change their image as needed to avoid prosecution. They also readily change their life story.

Other Related Qualities:

- Contemptuous of those who seek to understand them
- Do not perceive that anything is wrong with them
- Authoritarian
- Secretive
- Paranoid
- Very occasionally have difficulty with the law, but seek out situations where their tyrannical behavior will be tolerated, condoned, or admired
- Conventional appearance
- Goal of enslavement of their victim(s)
- Exercise despotic control over every aspect of the victim's life
- Has an emotional need to justify their crimes and therefore needs their victim's affirmation (respect, gratitude, and love)
- Ultimate goal is the creation of a willing victim
- Incapable of real human attachment to another
- Unable to feel remorse or guilt
- Extreme narcissism and grandiose

(The above traits are based on the psychopathy checklists of H. Cleckley and R. Hare.)

After reading this checklist, Desi decided to purchase Dr. Hare's Books and began to research further and to read everything about the subject. She read whatever she could get her hands on. Desiree kept going over this material in her mind. It kept her up sometimes into all hours of the night. Desiree was disturbed by what she had read. She continued to weigh these facts and to try to make them not fit. Surely, he loved her, 'I am not that big a fool am I?'

Repeated lying, it said. They live for the moment. They do not plan ahead and are very impulsive. They appear to be charming, at times. They have relationships, in name only and they end them when it suits them. They have the innate ability to find ones weaknesses and are more than ready to use them. They do it to fulfill their own needs, by deceiving; manipulating and intimidation, and they enjoy it. They do not have true emotions of any kind. They do not keep jobs that last long because they become bored easily. They may get upset but they quickly let it go. There is no cure for this disorder. They sometimes use an alias. They rationalize the pain that they inflict. They play a part to get what they want. Their only goal is self-gratification. No one can say 'a psychopath could not fool me.'

The words kept playing repeatedly in her head, Think you can spot one? Think again. They see themselves as victims. How can that be? Although, all alone in her bed in the middle of the night, Desiree questioned these words aloud. She continued to toss and turn and to think. Zach always told her, "You think too much." Heaven forbid, a woman who thinks. The last thing Zach wanted was a woman who thinks; she continued to read.

It is impossible to prevent ourselves from becoming friends or lovers to a sociopath. They switch jobs as frequently as they do lovers and are usually stringing several along at the same time. They gain your affection quickly. They disarm you with words and intrigue you with grandiose plans.

They use your friends and the information they accumulated during your relationship to try to ruin your reputation, your job and, your life when it is over. Notify your friends and family. Make certain everyone knows what is going on. Inform the police, including federal agencies, even the criminal investigation division of the .I.R.S. and the F.B.I.

If they have money, they will probably not harm you but may try to have someone else do it. Do not try to explain; just move on. Because he/she is void of emotion, and has been playing with yours, you will appear to be the crazy one, while he is looking around, not reacting, as if he does not know what is wrong with you. He portrays normal better than normal does.

Sociopaths are the biggest users and takers we will encounter. They will likely come into our lives if we do not learn from less damaging life experiences. That is why boundaries are so important. Those with boundaries would see right through them. They would stop them before they began to break them down, emotionally. There are more than two million sociopaths in the United States, and the number is growing. Most are not murderers as we have been led to believe. However, the devastation they leave behind will make you wish you were dead.

Sociopaths can see you coming. They will seek you out. Once they have you hooked, your life will be, forever changed. They will take your trust and everything you stand for, and, in the end, use it to destroy you. They are extremely narcissistic, and have an ample supply of victims as their backup plan. They are always ready to move on when their double life is uncovered. The road back to sanity is long, but worth it.

If they show signs of having a serious personality disorder, get out while the going is good. Sociopaths have an uncanny ability to find people like the person she once was, and the innate ability to exert and maintain control. The outcome depends on how strong you are at your core. Do not explain. You will appear to be the crazy one; just move on.

Once again, Desiree had more questions than answers. Did she waste eight years? Did she know him at all? Was she in love with no one? The answer finally came to her; 'I do not know the answer and it really does not matter. The more time I spend on that question, the less time I have left.'

Only a psychiatrist is qualified to pass judgment, she thought. Maybe it was simply that greed had taken him down this road; they were certainly on two very different roads. It was not her position to judge or to make a diagnosis but she could now stand up and say, I know what I know, I heard what I heard, and I saw what I saw. What I know for sure is that he is not the right person for me.

In one respect, Desiree was relieved that she was not crazy, but at the same time deeply saddened to know that, she was in love with the image Zach presented. While she felt Zach could transform in to anything she wanted him to be to get what he wanted, he was not that image. There were still times when she missed the person she loved.

Zach stopped by to see Desiree at the end of July 2007, just days after Kylie quit and, three months after she asked him to leave. He pulled up in his truck in the back of her salon. She immediately noticed a bruise on his cheek.

"What happened to you?"

"Someone gave me some cabinets for one of the cottages. I was moving them and hit my cheek, no big deal." He continued,

"I guess I won't be leaving here until next April."

"Why's that?"

"When I'm finished with the building for the trucking company, I'm building a bar near Sauk Village and a strip mall near St. John." When Zach landed a big job, it was usually through one of his affluent friends. He would then use that job to make it appear that he is a big contractor.

"Who are you doing that for?"

"Oh, some girl from Cedar Lake."

Knowing who and what he is, she smiled.

"How'd that happen, Zach?"

"She was driving passed the trucking company and stopped. She liked what she saw; it just sort of fell in my lap. I didn't put up a sign specifically for that reason."

She laughed and dropped it thinking to herself, 'if only he had body parts as large as his ego, I probably would not have dumped him.' He left, however that was nowhere close to the last time Desiree would see him. She saw him more now than when he lived with her.

In early August, two weeks after he stopped by, she was speaking to one of her clients. Desiree was telling him what Zach had told her,

"You know he met her in a bar somewhere."

He announced,

"That's in today's paper."

"What is?"

"The girl from Cedar Lake who's building the bar near Sauk Village, her name is Dee Klawinski; she owns Here's to You. The paper said she's a developer." Desiree was right all along.

She could not believe what she was hearing, but it all made sense to her now. Every time they broke up, he was immediately involved with someone who was either a developer, or in a similar position. Zach had already been somehow involved with these women and when he and Desi would break up, he would simply date them out in the open.

Desiree explained to him about Zach being in Dee's bar while she was in Florida. "Desiree there is something seriously wrong with that dude and he will never change. He has always been this way; I bet that he did this to his wife too. I would put money on it."

Chapter 36

He was her last client on Saturday and Desiree went to the gas station to buy the newspaper. After she read it, she drove to 'Here's to You.' She needed closure. She sat down at the bar and ordered a drink. The bar was somewhat of a dive but she had heard the food was good. It was just over the state line in Lynwood. She had suspected long ago that he was going to bars there to do "business."

As Desiree looked around and watched the servers and the bartender she thought maybe this was, just business. Everyone had dark hair and from experience, she knew if he were seeing someone there, she would have blonde in her hair. Then she walked behind the bar from the backroom.

She went to the computer and asked one of the girls to turn the music down. She was entering an order in the computer and she seemed to feel Desiree staring. Her hair was the same as Desi's; it had the same texture and was highlighted as hers was. It struck her that she was the only attractive blonde there. The other girls were somewhat plain and had dark hair. She stood out; Desiree could not help but wonder if that was the plan.

Desiree wondered if; all of his "business partners" were in one room, would look like sisters? The only thing that set Desiree apart from the others was the fact that they had money and she did not. They seemed to be free spirits and more social, while Desiree liked to have fun, she was a homebody and a mom. She was a salon owner, as was his wife; and Desiree fit the appearance criteria he looked for. Was she simply revenge because she owned a salon? They were also the same size. Dee was younger, in her upper forties, pretty with a very nice smile.

She stopped what she was doing, turned, and looked directly at Desiree. She probably felt her staring.

"Hello," she said.

"Hi."

Desiree was trying to decide, 'do I leave this picture of Zach and me, or do I just display some class and leave' – she left.

For the first time since Desiree ended their relationship, she contacted Zach. She sent him a text.

"Zach if you're in town please call, if you're out of town please call when you get here. It's important."

Around noon on Sunday, Zach called,

"Hey, what's going on?"

"Can we get together for a few minutes; I need to talk to you?"

"Did you get yourself in trouble again?"

She knew he was referring to the debt she had incurred building the salon, after their 'Julianna' break-up.

She decided to play to his ego, he had taught her well.

"No, I'm leaving for Florida again soon and I have some issues I need to resolve." I thought who better to help me with that than you."

After driving by and following her constantly, he suddenly needs to think about whether he could fit her in or not.

"Well, maybe later this afternoon, let me check. I'll call you later."

She knew him well enough to know; he hung up and immediately called Dee to see if the cat was out of the bag.

Within five minutes, he called back.

"I have to go to Schererville to get my truck washed anyway, so I'll stop by your place."

"I would rather meet you somewhere else." Jake was home and Zach's disappearances had devastated him.

"Okay, have you had lunch?" he asked.

226

"No, I haven't."

"Meet me at Schoops in 30 minutes."

She was there in 30 minutes; he was there in 45. He was going to make her wait. He was letting Desiree know she was no longer important enough for him to be on time. She got it. They sat in a booth and as always, ordered their lunch and the small talk came easy.

He began telling her how well his life was going and Desiree just let him talk.

"I'm going to buy 53 acres on the lake in Wisconsin."

"Really, why?"

"I'm going to subdivide it and build myself a place right on the lake. I am also planning to build a log house on my 80 acres. It will make the value go way up should I decide to sell it."

"I thought you said you'd never sell it."

He replied,

"Everything is for sale."

"I thought you were going to buy the Marina," she added.

"Oh, I will probably do that too."

"Wow, Zach."

As he looked down toward the floor, he said,

"Things are really looking up for me." He slowly raised his head to look at her with a smile,

"I mean things are really looking up." She just let him talk, another riddle.

"Good for you, Zach."

"Enough about me. What about you?"

"Well as always Zach when we get together to talk, everything seems to leak from my brain; give me a minute."

As he stood to go to the restroom, he said,

"If it's important you will remember it, I'll be right back."

She gathered her thoughts and her composure so she would be ready when he came back. He sat down across from her, intently looking into her eyes. Desiree could not help but to think back to the day he told her,

"Don't let Duke stare at you, he is trying to establish and maintain control."

Desiree broke his stare and looked away.

"Zach, do you remember when I was in Florida a few months ago, the end of April and you told me that you wanted to be married to me?"

"Yes and I meant that too."

"You did not!" Desiree allowed a minute to pass; she did not want him to leave just yet.

"Do you remember telling me a couple of weeks ago, that you were going to build a bar near Sauk Village for some girl from Cedar Lake. She stopped by, liked what she saw, and asked you to build it; it just fell in your lap. You even commented that you did not put a sign up for that very reason, remember telling me that?" He nodded. "Remember when I was in Florida, I called and asked you where you were, and you said, "A bar in Lynwood, and when I asked you what bar, you kept repeating, just a bar in Lynwood and finally you said, Here's to You."

"mmhmm."

"Well, I was talking to one of my clients the other day and he told me, the girl you are building for is Dee Klawinski." He nodded.

"Guess what, Zach?" She paused while he stared,

"She owns Here's to You."

The untrained eye would have never noticed his disgust, but Desiree did. He seemed to love throwing out one riddle after another but felt he was too smart for anyone to decipher one, and it really pissed him off when that happened. He seemed to derive great pleasure from her pain.

"So what" he retorted.

"So tell me Zach, Were you dating her in April, while you were asking me to marry you?"

"Na, we just started dating about a month ago." Remembering it was only two weeks prior when he said, "some girl from Cedar Lake." He was dating her at the time.

Desiree's heart knew but at the same time, it sank into the pit of her stomach. He continued,

"The day you called me from Florida was the first day we met. She had buried her father that day and I went with Keith to her bar; they had a dinner there after his funeral."

That was not true and she knew it, unless he met her long before she went to Florida. Either way he was lying. Why would he go to a dinner after someone's funeral when he did not know her or her family? He did not even go to her mother's funeral.

Desiree was in Florida the end of April and she had heard Dee's father had passed away the beginning of March. When she confronted him about that, instead of showing guilt or shame about being caught in a bold-faced lie, with no remorse he calmly said,

"I did not meet her until long after that. I met her when I went with Keith to deliver papers to her, and we did not start dating until months after you and I split."

Desiree heard Brianna's voice whispering to her, "He has an answer for everything, doesn't he."

'He's good at what he does,' she thought. Jim her client and friend of many years had remarked,

"Boy, he must be talented."

"Not in the place you are thinking Jim, his talent is up here," As she pointed to her head. Zach was not so much intelligent as he was living off instinct, as an animal would, with no conscience.

"Des, I have known him for years. He is not treating you any differently than he did Sheila."

Desiree was incredulous. How can he smoothly go from one lie to another without skipping a beat? He does not flinch, squirm and does not pause. Desiree knew Keith was not working; he had been fired from the family business. Zach was building a new building for the trucking company for him at that time.

"Good luck with that. I wish you the best, because if I did not, it would mean I never loved you. I must tell you though I went to her bar. I needed to see for myself. I assure you I will never go back. I did not stay long. My intention was not to bother her, just to prove to myself what I already knew."

"I want you to go where ever you want. I don't care if you go there."

"I must say, she's a pretty girl, Zach."

He responded,

"She's not bad."

He leaned over the booth, looked directly into Desiree's eyes, and smiled,

"But then again I don't date ugly women."

Beneath her demure smile Desiree was thinking, 'you are one arrogant, egotistical son of a bitch.'

"I wish you the best, Zach."

"I'm just going to see where it goes" he replied. 'You mean, ride the ride, right Zach.' She smiled at her own interpretation of what he had just said.

"Tell me something, are you going to make money from her?"

Without hesitation,

"You bet your ass I am, this time next year I'm going fishing. Then again, you know me, I live moment to moment; I am just going to see where it goes."

"You never took money from me, so I was just wondering," She added.

"Well, things have changed," he shot back.

"I guess I shouldn't have told you so often how good looking you were."

He smiled,

"I knew I was good looking long before I ever met you. You are family oriented and, I am not. You like two read books and I always have to have something going on."

Desi thought, 'Those are two perfect reasons for ending an eight year relationship, what took so long?' She had always heard, what brings you together will be the very thing that breaks you up. She remembered when they first began dating, him saying,

"I've never been this relaxed in my life; it's so peaceful when I am with you."

"Are you ready to go?"

"Yes I am but give me one moment please; this will be the last time we meet."

For the first time his anger became visible.

"I don't understand why we can't continue to do what we are doing right now, you are so old fashioned."

"Zach you are dating and I don't think Dee would appreciate you hanging out with your ex-fiancé. By the way it's also inappropriate for you to follow me, come to the salon for a haircut or to visit."

"Well, I guess I should just take your number out of my phone." Desiree just looked at him, but did not respond.

"Yours…and…Jake's." Now he is playing that card.

"Zach, why do you have our numbers in your phone?"

"Just in case. If you do not want me to acknowledge you in public, I won't. You need to think about it."

He paid for lunch and they left. Desiree could not help thinking; 'I hope all of this goes bottoms up.'

She texted him later, "Zach, I have thought about what you said and my answer is no, do not acknowledge me. I am happy for you but it is time for me to find someone to be in my life too. Good luck, I wish you the best."

Did she wish him the best, no not really; Desiree truly hoped Dee was using him. She believed he might have met his match. Many times, Desiree plotted some sort of revenge, only to come to her senses and allow "karma" to take its course. She hoped when he got what was coming to him, that she would not care one way or the other.

Kylie suddenly announced that she quit; they had been so close. She had been behaving strangely for a few months. Finally in late July, and a few days before Zach made his first visit, she came to Desiree and said,

"I can't take it anymore." She was crying.

Zach would drive by, stop in to see her and it seemed she felt intimidated and now she knew why. Kylie lived in Lynwood and frequented 'Here's to You.' His two worlds were about to collide.

Dolores came in for her usual Wednesday morning appointment and could not wait to tell Desiree she saw Kylie at a funeral.

"She's working at some salon in Highland, right behind K-Mart." Desiree could not believe what she was hearing. What are the odds that the girl Zach so desperately wanted out of her salon would end up at New Dimensions Salon, working for Yancy?

When Dolores left, she texted Zach,

"When you start damning my character and messing with my business you are directly hurting Jake and that is not going to happen. Unlike Sheila, I am not afraid of you."

Within the hour, the salon got a private phone call; they just held the phone. A handsome man came in, looked around, made an appointment for the next evening, and then never showed up. The following morning Desi was late for work. When she arrived, a car from Illinois was sitting in her parking space. She parked two cars away. When she got out of, unlike most guys who would look at anything wearing a skirt, he did not turn his head; he just stared toward Route 41.

She went back and forth to her car several times to get some things from the trunk; he never looked at her. The only time she saw him look was when she decided to lock the salon. She saw him looking at her through his side view mirror. He stayed for two and a half hours. Why she did not phone the police was a mystery even to her.

The following morning, and several thereafter, at the precise time Desiree parked her car, Zach pulled up to the light directly in front of her; she could almost reach out and touch his truck. He wanted her to know he was behind this but was careful not to cross the line.

He is brilliant, she thought, in an evil sort of way. Desiree knew when she repeated this to someone who only knew him casually; they would think she was as crazy as Zach had tried to convince her she was. The more she tried to explain, the more frustrated she became and the crazier she looked, she felt. While in the meantime he seemed to have no emotion or conscience and was able to calmly, walk away shaking his head saying, "What is wrong with that girl?" Where had she heard that before?

Her father use to say that, as she flashed back to when she was 10 years old. One evening he came home and Desi's arm was wrapped in bandages, compliments of the ten stitches she had received while he was gone. Braden had inflicted that wound with a metal xylophone earlier that day. Then there was the time, early one morning when Desi had heard their phone ring. It was located in her mom and dad's room. She went running in there, obviously not thinking; when she got the shock of her life; at least up to that point. It was a hot August morning and with no air conditioning, they were naked; an image she was horrified to see, and would never forget. As Desiree was exiting the room as quickly as she could get her skinny little legs to move, she heard her dad say,

"What is wrong with that girl?"

She spoke to several police officer friends, as well as an FBI friend, and a States Attorney.

"Desiree, there is no doubt he is behaving strangely, and with some of the things you have told me I wouldn't believe you if I didn't know what kind of person you are. The truth is; on the surface he is doing nothing wrong, these are public streets and the places he is showing up in and you just 'happen to be there,' while I know it is not a coincidence, it is legal. Unfortunately, unless he does something to you, there is not much we can do. However, having said that, these kinds of people usually live on the edge of the law. You can always contact the IRS or the FBI if he does continue."

"He has taken enough of my time; I just want him to leave me alone. If anything should happen to me, remember whom to look for. He will not do it himself; he will have someone else do it. He thinks he is too smart to be caught."

She mourned the death of the dream Zach promised. She realized it was her dream, not his.

She knew this was not all about Zach, this was about her, and Desiree planned to take time to work on herself. Zach could not have used her if she had not allowed it. Desiree recalled a conversation she had with her client friend Shel.

"Des, you wear your heart on your sleeve, and you need to tuck it in a little bit."

Chapter 37

Desiree accomplished what was most important to her, raising her three beautiful children. She did the best she could.

That summer went quicker than she thought it would. Desiree was over Zach but not the damage he had done. He had buried himself deep within her psyche. Only time and a lot of patience among friends and family would mend it.

Zach was not her knight in shining armor, nor was his big white truck, the white horse she dreamed she would ride in someday with her prince to take her away, and live happily, ever after.

He was a figment of her wild imagination, and she was in love with who she believed he was, and who he represented himself to be, and not who he truly is.

He did not have the capability to love anyone but himself. He allowed his love of money, his good looks, charm, and most of all, his ego to destroy what God had given him.

For him, life is nothing more than a chess game; he speaks in riddles, and is the king while everyone he surrounds himself with are nothing more than pawns he discards when they are no longer useful. As for Jake, Zach completely walked out of his life. There are no more calls to take, neither Christmas gifts, nor any calls at all, no birthday cards, no visits, or gifts in the mail. So much for the son he never had.

Zach shows up everywhere she goes. Head games she thinks he called it. Remembering a conversation Zach had with Jake over dinner one evening,

"Jake, women want what they can't have, never forget that." Zach did not give advice much, his theory seemed to be live and let live. Desiree explained to Jake while this is sometimes true, it is not always the case. She for one never chased what she felt she could not have. That was a game and she did not play games.

"Men are offenders of this rule also."

During that same dinner he mentioned he had to go back North; he had work to do. Desiree was disappointed that he was leaving, and he laughed.

"Jake your Mom thinks we can live on love, isn't that sweet."

He sometimes shows up in different cars, such as the expensive black convertible sports car he pulled up, sideways in front of her door. When Desiree glanced up, Zach then drove away. His friend Matthew had owned one like it, and she assumed he had borrowed it. Zach had taken her for a ride in Matthew's just after Reagan passed away.

Zach knew that material things did not impress her; but evidently, they do impress him. How many times had she told him, good character, integrity, honesty, and morals are the things of which she was impressed? 'Amazing,' she thought, 'How well he is doing, when only a couple of years ago he was working at Lowes, let go at the construction company and then living on unemployment for a year.'

It was now July 2008, over a year since she ended their relationship, and he was continuing to play his game. A male friend had taken Desiree out for a leisurely ride in his black T-Bird convertible just two weeks prior when they passed Zach.

Someone told her the black sports car he was driving belonged to Dee. She had just traded her SUV in, and bought it.

'Could he already have so much power and control over her, and manipulated her in to doing this?' Surely, he would not go that far just to upset her. Laughing to herself while thinking, 'I do not care if she has a Lamborghini, but I do hope she has a GPS tracker.'

Thinking back on where she came from, material things did not mean much to her. Because money and material things impress him, Desiree guessed he acts on the theory everyone is impressed as well.

When she saw him in Dee's car, she saw no pride, no integrity, no manliness; she saw a child; a child showing off someone else's success. A success he has never been able to achieve, and is now using her to achieve it.

Desiree was happy with the things she had and most of all, her peace of mind. Something Zach is desperately trying to prevent, and certainly does not possess.

He would like nothing more than for her to be miserable without him. He would enjoy watching her business fail, and has tried to see that it does. That is one reason, why Kylie leaving was so important to him.

Desiree was speaking to a good friend.

"What if he tries to hurt you? Better yet, have someone else hurt you. You know he thinks he is smarter than everyone else and believes he wouldn't get caught."

Desiree replied,

"You mean what if he kills me? He has already done that over and over again. He has too much to lose and much bigger fish to fry. Besides, everyone in my circle knows what he has done, and even some in his circle of friends knows, Matthew and Al, the good old boys. He would never get away with it. You do not know how many times I have wanted to call Dee to warn her. She is a successful businessperson; you would think she could see through him by now."

"Listen to you. You are an attractive and intelligent woman, and it took you eight years to figure him out. Think about it, he is playing to women's egos. If she is attractive and smart, she believes that is why he wants her. As time goes on, she will continue trying to make it work so that she does not look like a fool. Isn't that what you did? He will use his long marriage and your long relationship to sell her on theirs. Isn't that what he does in business, with big jobs? He used the only big job he has ever had, the trucking company to sell Dee on him. He works his relationships the same way he does his jobs; Pretty simple."

"How could I have been so stupid?"

"You are not stupid, you were in love. Des, do you remember all of the horrible things he told you about Sheila? Don't you think he has told Dee nasty things about you too? She would never believe you, that is how he gets by with it. Let her find out on her own just like you had to."

"I found out the hard way and I hate to see other women get hurt while I stand back and do nothing about it."

"Maybe she is using him, you don't know; we can only hope."

If Desi is outside, Zach goes through the drive through, and stops and talks. He asked her one day why she had not stayed longer at Angelo's so he could buy her a drink, and how he had been 'working his dick off.' Laughing, the thought crossed her mind, 'I am surprised it hasn't rotted off by now.'

"He is a piece of shit Des, let it go." She remembered a conversation she had recently had with a client who had known Zach for years, and who was an acquaintance of Dee's. "I told you a long time ago, he has done this for years. Sometimes people believe the grass is greener on the other side until they get there, then they have regrets."

"That is sad, and it makes me want to cry."

"Don't be sad, and I don't want to make you cry. You can rise above this; you are a better person than that."

"Zach told me in the beginning of our relationship, "Never trust anyone, totally.""

"I guess I trusted too much."

"You cannot trust too much, you just chose the wrong person to trust, that's all."

She fell in love, she gave everything, and he took it all.

Chapter 38

Desiree did see Rafael again.

It was Saturday, her last day in Siesta Key in September 2007, and the day after Zach called "accidentally." She was packed and ready to leave early on Sunday morning to catch her flight. She took her shower, put on her PJs and laid down.

She always had a difficult time sleeping the night before she left home and the one before she left to go home. It was around 10 pm when she heard her cell phone ringing. She hurried to answer it; 'it must be one of my boys.' The ringing stopped by the time she got to her phone. Desiree looked at caller id and was surprised to see a Florida call. She did not recognize the number.

She called her sister Raquel, told her what happened and had to admit she was a little uneasy. She asked for the number and said she would call back. Less than a minute later, she called and said,

"It was a foreign guy and there was loud music in the background, I hung up when he answered the phone."

"It had to be Rafael calling. I'm going down there to talk to him, for all I know Zach might have him watching me." 'Now I am becoming paranoid,' she thought.

"Maybe someone saw you and told him that you were in town."

"Maybe, but I'm going to find out."

Raquel stayed on the phone while she made the short walk to Blasé. Desiree reached for the door, opened it and he was the first person she saw. She closed the door,

"He's here but I cannot go in, I don't have on any make-up." She went back styled her hair, put on her face and headed back.

She walked in, ordered a drink, and took it out on the deck. There was no one outside so she had her choice of tables. Within a couple of minutes a guy came out and introduced himself,

"Hi, I am Jeff, and you are?"

"Desiree."

He began telling her about his business, how he chartered boats, when another guy came out and sat at the next table. Thinking to herself, 'boy people are sure friendly around here.'

"They call me Ralphie. I am the chef." Desiree continued to explain to Jeff about the call she had received and rattled off the number.

"I think that is Rafael's number, let me check."

He went inside, leaving her to hear Ralphie's story, how he was Italian, from New York, unlucky in the love department, had been married four times, and had several children. As she was trying to figure out how he could possibly support that many families on a chef's salary and still live here, Jeff came to the door and nodded his head; it was indeed Rafael's number.

Ralphie continued to talk and she was catching about every third sentence when Rafael came out on the deck. She overheard him ask someone,

"Why is Jeff asking me what my phone numbel is?" He shrugged and went back inside.

About five minutes later, he came back out and sat in a single chair on the deck next to the door. She knew he wanted to speak to her but Ralphie was on a roll, and she was trying not to be rude.

He got up and went back inside. He waited about five more minutes and came out; realizing Ralphie was never going to shut up.

This time he walked directly to her table,

"I know you."

"I met you when I was here in April, do you remember me?"

"I did not folget the night on the beach."

Ralphie began talking to a guy that was leaving the bar.

"You wele so sad, you had been in a vely bad lelationship, I lemembel evely detail." Desiree told him she felt this had been set up. She explained that her ex had been stalking her, so she was confused about who might have set it up.

He was quiet for a moment and then looked at her and smiled,

"You mean if you knew it wasn't him you would have done mole." she smiled back. They said good-bye and she left.

Chapter 39

Seven months had gone by; April 2008 and here she was, leaving once again for Siesta Key. Desiree could not afford this trip and to be honest she could not afford any of these vacations. However, they allowed her the opportunity to write; it was one thing she loved to do. She felt she could not afford not to take them.

Zach came to the Smoke Shop every day for a week prior to her leaving. She assumed someone told him she was leaving. Her client jokingly said,

"If he keeps that up you won't have to worry, he'll be dead from lung cancer." Melissa, The stylist who replaced Kylie told her he did not come once while she was gone.

Desiree let it go. Her sister Raquel wanted to go this time. Desiree was used to being on her own but on the positive side; she would have someone to go with for dinner and they could spend some time together.

The weather could not have been better, 85 degrees every day, and 70s at night, and with the breeze from the Gulf, it was perfect. They shopped and drove around a lot more than she would have on her own; however, she discovered new places.

Desiree and Raquel went to have lunch with their aunts twice. Noreen and Joy were their dad's two sisters and Aunt Beth, their grandmother's sister. Desiree felt so connected to them. Desi and Raquel took pictures and asked many questions, trying to learn as much about the family as they could. That was probably the highlight of their stay.

Aunt Joy and Aunt Noreen took them to two different places on the water. Raquel had never met two of them and Desiree was happy for her that she finally did. It was another piece of their history she could add to her life.

They later ventured down to the village for dinner at Maximo's. They sat out on the deck, enjoyed good food, Shrimp Gorgonzola, Desi's favorite, good conversation, and beautiful weather at the same time. As Desiree took it all in, she thought 'maybe this is heaven'.

After dinner, curiosity got the better of her. She wanted to go to Blasé to see if Rafael was there. When they sat down, he came right over,

"Hi, how ale you." He sat down and the first thing he asked was,

"How is yol life going?"

"I am very happy with my life now."

Others were talking as he asked,

"What does this mean?"

Desiree's attention went in another direction and she did not get the chance to respond. At one point Raquel looked at her and said,

"You know, I know he is too young for you and this sounds crazy but you two look as though you belong together."

Raquel asked,

"Rafael, will you take a picture of me with my sister?"

"I vil take a pictule of you with youl sistel, if you vil take a pictule with me and youl sistel." They enjoyed the evening, meeting people from all over the country.

The way the bar was designed, the bartenders could come to the outside bar from the inside bar. She was standing in front of the outside bar when Rafael walked behind it. He was looking behind the bar for something, and with his head still pointing down, his eyes looked up, "Vhat?"

"Nothing, I'm just looking, can't a girl just look?"

"Sometimes it is betel to do mole than just look." She could have sworn the temperature went up 10 degrees, and the entire week went that way.

However, toward the end of the week and although he was very protective and continued to kiss her every time she went, he backed off somewhat.

On Friday, they went to Blasé to see Rafael one last time. They were leaving on Sunday and she wanted to thank him. Desiree knew why he was in her life; she had no grand illusions about a future, he had become her friend. He took the time to notice her pain and he told Desiree,

"Thel is much betel out thel fol you."

He was 31, very handsome, and while most are selfish at that age, he gave of himself when he could have been doing many other things.

He wandered over to their table, kissed Desiree, extended his cheek for Raquel to kiss, and then ran back in the bar. He stopped by as he was waiting on customers and when he leaned over to kiss her cheek, she whispered,

"Can I have five minutes of your time, before I go?"

"You galt it."

Ralphie came out and sat with them,

"Hey got any pot on you?" She had never smoked pot in her life and did not believe in her 52 years that she had ever been asked that question. He was rambling and she said,

"I am sorry, I forgot your name."

"Ralphie is my nickname. No one can pronounce my real name I'm from New York, I'm Italian" Here we go again, she interrupted,

"Ralphie, like in A Christmas Story?"

"Ya, I'll shoot your F----- eye out."

Desiree thought she was going to pee her pants, she was laughing so hard. She excused herself and headed to the restroom. The restaurant was closed, however you had to go through it to get to the restrooms, so there was dim lighting on the walls.

Desiree was still laughing when she came out and as she made her way through the restaurant, she saw Rafael coming in. The room was dark and empty; only the two of them; standing there. The laughter turned into a smile as he walked toward Desiree. He pulled out empty chairs from a table, one for Desiree, and one for him. Time seemed to stand still and there was dead silence in the room. He waited for her to sit and then he sat down.

He sat in front of Desiree, so close their knees were touching. He leaned toward her face and in almost a whisper he asked,

"Vhat do you vant to say to me?"

Desiree could not help but to answer in the same low tone,

"I just wanted to say, thank you."

He raised his hands and rested his palms on each cheek as he pulled her toward him and gently kissed her on the lips.

He pulled back only a few inches and said,

"Don't you evel folget vhat a beautiful voman you ale." Desiree's embarrassment must have shown.

"I am not kitting you, you ale a beautiful voman."

She responded,

"Rafael if you ever need anything, feel free to call me."

"I have youl numbel."

"I will be back in September."

He got up and walked away. She began walking faster to catch up with him.

"I plobably won't be hele."

"What do you mean, you probably won't be here?" He continued to walk, no longer making eye contact, she understood him to say something about the "Govelment."

He went back to the bar while she went back to the deck. Raquel was sitting there with a puzzled look on her face. Desiree sat down smiled and said,

"He says; I am beautiful." As if, she had never heard that phrase before.

About that time, Rafael came bursting through the doors next to their table and continued talking as if their conversation had not ended. Raquel's mouth was gaped open with the same puzzled look as if to say,

'What is going on?'

He looked over at her,

"I came to this countly alone, and I knew no one. I had no self-esteem, I was in a hollible lelationshp. I have made many fliends and you ale one. All it takes is to say one nice thing, ol do one nice thing fol someone," as if he were demonstrating an inch with his fingers,

"It doesn't have to be a big thing, all it takes is one small thing, and you could change someone's life."

That would not be the last time Desiree saw Rafael.

Some people she felt come in your life, not to stay but for a reason. The difficult part was recognizing it and letting go.

Desiree believed Zach was a master of deception, and the king of manipulation.

She was not a good partner in the dance of deception. Yes, she would always ask Zach, "Do you wanna dance?"

He would always reply, "Sweetie I am dancing." Little did she know, he was.

Zach lived for the moment, and she believed one should live in the moment; there is a big difference. Desiree does not look too far ahead – there is no promise of tomorrow, and all she has is now.

She agreed with one thing Zach said to her, "Enough about me, what about you?" Desiree was part of the game and she could not fix him.

Desiree recalled her own words,

"You have a long road ahead of you, and I don't want to go down that road."

His words from the beginning came to the surface of her mind, "I can juggle, just wait you will see."

Desiree is continually finding pennies from heaven. Not all of them are heads up, but when they are, she picks them up and tucks them in her purse, looks up, smiles, and says,

"I love you Mom, thanks."

Desiree Peters is foot loose and fancy free!

Epilogue

Desiree began doing for herself what Zach had done in the beginning. She indulged herself in the little things. She bought herself flowers; she always had flowers.

Grace had inflicted emotional and physical pain on her children; she did not know any better. While Desiree was determined not to inflict the same pain upon her children, she inflicted emotional pain upon herself.

At the same time, while making poor choices in her personal life, she inadvertently inflicted emotional pain on her own children. She now understood her mother.

Even now, Zach continues to try to maintain his power and control by driving by. He continues to come to the Smoke Shop, next door to her salon, several times a week. If Desiree were outside, he would go to the drive through and stop to talk, and then disappear. He follows her to the grocery store, and then disappears. He follows her to the Post Office, pulling her off the road to talk, and then disappears. He follows her to the bank, Wal-Mart as well as into bars and restaurants where he makes a point of sitting across from her and, then disappears; at least for a while.

He calls her 'accidentally' and anonymously. Zach knew the disappearing acts would make her curious and anticipate his next visit. He was testing her strength and every time she walked away with no contact on her part, she was getting stronger while his hold was becoming weaker.

She was no longer dependent on him. Zach thrived on her dependence.

He never raises his voice and always maintains his disguise. It is one of kindness and class. He is well spoken, "private" and very quiet. Do not mistake his quietness for being shy he is not shy. He is sitting back assessing your vulnerabilities and needs. If you are going through any crisis such as a death in your family or you simply 'need' his help, he moves in. He now knows exactly what to do, and how to do it. He is always one or two steps ahead of where he is, and knows exactly what he is doing. He is always setting up his backup plan, the next "chess game."

He will use you for many reasons, the number one being money. If you have money, that is great, but if you are a developer with money – that is even better, you provide jobs. If you are a developer with money and a home for him to live in when he comes to town, your chances of being with him are even greater. If you are blonde, thin, pretty, and have all of the above, and you provide sex; you are his ultimate goal, pawn, and victim.

There had been many developers in the past several years; however, Dee was the only one who took the bait. Everyone told Desi,

"She is using him."

"He may allow her to believe she is using him; however he is in control."

It was September 2007, and the day after she closed her journal, when Zach called.

She was parking her rented, baby blue Mustang to have lunch with her Aunt Joy, when she answered the phone. Desiree was relaxed and did not look at caller id. "Hello."

That familiar voice said,

"Dave, please."

"Who?" she asked.

"Dave." she was so frustrated, thinking this was never going to end.

"Zach, you have reached Desiree."

In the familiar soft voice, she had heard so many times before he responded, "I ... am...so...sorry." Click. When she returned home, Cassie told her,

"Oh by the way, Zach called."

"What did he want?"

"He left a message asking if we wanted a basketball court for the kids. We didn't call him back." He continues to "accidentally" call and he continues to show up wherever she goes.

Summer was over and her favorite season was upon them. Time just simply flies.

Desiree kept herself busy and focused and before she knew it, it was winter of 2007. She decided she had been in hiding long enough. Suzanne, a girl she had gone to high school with, called to see if she would go out with her to North Star's, to listen to a band play.

She came early and mentioned she would like to go by the Quest to see if some of the guys she knew would be there. Desiree said,

"I have not seen Zach for about six weeks, I guess we can go, he's probably back in Wisconsin."

She pulled in the parking lot, did not see his truck, so they parked and went in. When she walked through the door, Zach was sitting at the bar talking to a man next to him and as if a magnet, his head turned and he looked directly at her.

He nonchalantly turned back as if he had not seen her and continued to talk. Desiree was not about to leave. She waited this long to move on. She was here and she was not leaving.

There were three empty barstools, all of which were next to him. Desiree sat in the farthest one from him, as she said hello to her old friend, who was now working there.

251

Zach turned and looked straight ahead, not taking his eyes off the TV that was directly in front of him.

She noticed he looked depressed. It was his birthday, and it seemed rather pathetic he was sitting alone at the bar. Desiree told Denise to get him a drink for his birthday, and she did. She felt enough time had passed and it was the proper thing to do.

She went to the restroom and when she came back, he leaned back on his barstool and said,

"Thanks, Des."

"You're welcome, Zach, Happy Birthday." He seemed depressed to her.

"It's just another day," he replied. Desiree smiled and turned to continue her conversation.

The guy next to Desiree was trying to strike up a conversation while Denise and Desiree were trying to catch up on each other's lives.

She felt strong and in control, while at the same time feeling sad for what could have been. Zach's girlfriend, Dee called him, and all she heard him say was,

"What's that?" as though he could not hear what she said, and then his voice raised loud enough so as she could hear him,

"Oh, okay baby" and he hung up the phone. Denise shot him the 'I cannot believe you just said that,' look.

It stung a little; he had called Desiree baby for eight years, but she was surprised at how well she took it and it made her realize how insignificant his words were.

They stayed a little longer, she wished Denise a Happy New Year, and Desiree turned her back to Zach, and walked out.

Two days later, on December 31 2007 New Years Eve, she went to the post office to mail some bills. The salon was not open, but Melissa wanted to come in to take care of a few clients.

Desiree left her there and promised she would be back.

She pulled up to the stop sign, and as she was turning right, she noticed someone in a gray and black Honda sitting at the stop sign to her right, with his window down and his hand up gesturing for her to stop.

When she rounded the corner, she saw Zach. That must be why she did not know he was at the Quest; she had never seen this car before. That is why she did not see him for six weeks as well.

Desiree stopped, and he said,

"Where are you going?"

"I'm going to the Post Office."

"When you're finished meet me in Aldi's parking lot."

She pulled into the post office, mailed her bills and left. Her gut told her to keep on driving and her heart wanted to stop; she stopped.

"I bought a new car. It will be paid for in a year."

She had recently seen a car exactly like his in her subdivision and the reason she noticed it was because many times Zach had mentioned that he wanted one.

"What do you want?"

"We should be able to talk when we see each other," he said.

"I had eight years invested in us."

"No you didn't Zach, you were too busy chasing women to get jobs. I have nothing to say to you, what would we have to talk about?"

"What has been going on in each other's lives for the past eight months, for starters?"

"Zach, you think you have traded up, don't you?"

The angrier she got, the calmer he became. He sat back in his seat, grabbed his bottle of water and calmly opened it, and began drinking.

"We'll see," he said,

"I am just going to see where it goes."

"No, Zach, we won't see, you can't find better."

Her phone was ringing, he said,

"Oh, that was me, I was behind you, trying to call you, but you did not answer."

That gave her the creeps; it did not make any sense. She wondered with his new car, just how long had he been following her and enjoying the fact that he was still conning her and getting by with it. The hair on the back of her neck stood up.

"It's Melissa."

"Who is Melissa?"

"She works for me, she replaced Kylie, and she knows you too."

"How?"

"You bought her and the entire bar a drink, at Benchwarmers."

"You know me; I would not spend that much money."

"Would you like to meet her, she's at the salon?"

"Sure."

He followed her back and into the salon. Melissa was shampooing her client,

"Zach, this is Melissa, Melissa, Zach." She looked up and said,

"I remember you; you bought me a drink at Benchwarmers once."

They spoke for a few minutes, she assured him she was not wrong and he conceded that maybe he had.

They went up front, leaving her to focus on her client when he commented on how nice the salon looked. They had added a few things, and he noticed. Zach was always good at details; she guessed you would have to be, to do what he does.

"Thanks for sending my mom a Christmas card," he said.

"I wanted to see her to say goodbye, I never got the chance, but I thought a note in her card was best."

"You should go see her; she's not doing very well."

"What's wrong?"

"She said she does not think she will be here next year, you should go see her if you want to."

She let that suggestion go, he looked down toward the floor, and in that gentle voice said, "I went to Mexico."

"What?"

He looked up, "I went to Mexico."

"That's nice Zach, you always promised to take me someplace, you never did, and now you are telling me, you took Dee to Mexico?"

"I didn't take her to Mexico."

"You didn't?"

"No," he paused, and looked up,

"She took me."

"She paid for your trip?"

"Sure, you don't think I would pay for that trip."

"That's nice Zach, how was it?"

"It was just Mexico, it was good to get away after finishing the building for the trucking company, and by the way, Keith is doing very well."

"That's good."

Desiree said goodbye to Melissa and headed for the door. Zach told Melissa it was nice to see her and followed her out.

"Have a Happy New Year."

"You too, Zach."

She went back to the Quest in March and a girl she knew yelled across the bar, "Your buddy just left," they laughed, and Desiree relaxed.

She was having lunch with an old client, Pat. Pat had to leave after an hour as her cat was being put down that night, and she was rather distraught.

They promised to get together and she left. Jackie her old partner from her first salon, and the one who yelled across the bar, asked if she would stay, and have a drink with her. Desiree accepted; life goes on and after all that they had been through; it was too short to let old wounds stand in their way.

As she made her way to the restroom, Zach walked through the door,

"Hey."

"Hey, Zach."

'He was just here an hour ago so why is he back?' she wondered.

Desiree went back to the bar. Jackie and Desiree had catching up to do. They spent about another hour catching up and reminiscing. Her sister, Shi was there and she joined in the conversation.

Zach sent drinks and they accepted them, but they were the last ones. They said their goodbyes, and left.

Zach still comes to the Smoke Shop two or three times a week. If Desiree is at the salon alone, he will sit there until she looks out, then he backs out and leaves.

She got an anonymous call on Christmas Eve. He followed her to the post office on New Year's Eve. The Tuesday, after her birthday and her first day back to work, as Desiree pulled in her parking spot, he pulled up next to her car. She was on the phone; he rolled down his window and moving his lips said,

"Happy Birthday."

He then waited for her to get off the phone, and yelled,

"Happy Birthday!" and drove away. She had just texted him the week before because he was calling her "accidentally" again. She asked him to delete her number and he promised he would. Now he is wishing her Happy Birthday.

Zach has begun building Dee's new bar. It will be located in the old vacant building across from the hospital where he and Desiree use to power walk, and across the street from the gym where she had worked out for years. She no longer goes to that part of town.

A lazy Sunday in May, Desiree decided to go to the grocery store to pick up a few things. She ran into Zach's good friend,

"Hi, Matthew, How are you?" He seemed puzzled.

"You don't know who I am, do you?"

'How soon they forget,' she was thinking, when he said,

"Take off those sunglasses."

256

"Desiree Peters."

"Oh, how are you?"

"Good and you?"

"Good."

"I apologize, you caught me on a bad day, and I look awful."

"So what, it's Sunday."

"Say hello to Lisa for me, it was nice to see you."

"I will, nice to see you too."

Desiree tried to find him again. She wanted to tell him to let Zach know that stalking was illegal. However, she did not run into him. She was there about fifteen minutes longer, grabbed a few more things and left. She loaded up her car and was on her way.

While waiting for the light to change, Desiree sat, back listening to her music, with the moon roof open, it was a nice day. She had learned long ago to relax in traffic. She would sing and dance or whatever she needed to do to take her mind off the heavy traffic.

She was looking around, when she saw a familiar arm hanging out of a car. They were waiting to turn into the parking lot she was leaving. She could only see his arm. She did not recognize the car. It was blue, and she thought it looked like a Toyota, probably a Camry.

Her mind drifted back to when she had met Zach for lunch last August; to tell him she knew about Dee, she mentioned she was car shopping, because Jake would be driving soon.

"I'm looking at Hondas," Desiree always knew he liked them, and she had heard good things about them.

"Don't get a Honda," he said, "they're not good cars anymore. You should get a Toyota, Camry." Zach had since purchased a Honda.

His light changed before hers, and sure enough, it was Zach. This took her back to the day when he told her he was sitting in Al's driveway when, while his truck was there, he was not.

It dawned on her he was not only using her, he was using his friends as well. How many times had she passed him and did not know it? How many times had he showed up in places she just happened, to be? How many times had she thought she saw him in cars, wearing a baseball cap? Only to think she must be crazy! Zach had never worn a baseball cap. She guessed he was playing a new role.

When she began 'investigating' him, he began leaving clues that would send her on a wild goose chase, while he was busy manipulating someone else. At the same time she was leading everyone in her circle and his to believe she was nuts.

When it was over, he could not only tell his friends and family about all of the crazy things she had done, but her friends would think she had lost it too. The best part for him is that the next girl would not believe any negative thing about him if word should get back to her. When he saw that she would not "stay out of his business," he began actively searching for her replacement.

Boy, Matthew must have called him before he left the store. Who owned the car he was driving – Matthews, Dee's, and who would believe that a man his age was spending that much time and effort to deceive? Who cares? It was brilliant in an evil sort of way.

Desiree realized that is how he gets away with it. No one in their right mind passed the age of 20 would do these things. With life as busy as it is who could imagine wasting so much precious time. She had, on him. Zach had no children, no commitments, and while he ran his jobs, he did not actually work unless he had to. He seemed to find boredom intolerable and had nothing but time on his hands. Zach was stalking just as a good hunter would. Desiree was once again reminded of something her mother said long ago,

"Desiree, it takes all kinds to make the world go around."

She called her sister, Brianna to see how her husband, Rob was doing. He recently had open-heart surgery and with all of his other health issues, she was concerned. She told her he was having problems breathing and his recovery was moving slowly. She asked what was going on with her.

Desiree told her she had been seeing Zach more now than when they lived together. Brianna replied,

"You know Des; I never understood how you of all people would allow anyone to treat you this way. Even when you were a little girl, you always stood up for yourself. You have always been independent and I believe you are the only person I know that even talked back to dad. You were so strong."

"It's difficult for me to understand too." Desi explained about what had happened at the grocery store. She mentioned, she did not recognize the car he was driving but oddly enough; she recognized his arm. Desiree went on further to explain, there was something about the way he was dangling his arm on the side of the car that drew her to it. Most people rest their arm on the door, and his was dangling down toward the street.

Brianna said in passing,

"Dad did that."

Desiree flashed back and although she was 11 when he passed, she felt a memory of that, and she replied,

"Of course he did."

Desiree was never going to be with a man like her dad but down to every detail, she did just that, from a double life with other women to even his mannerisms. Amazing, she thought. Desiree forgave her father and said good-bye.

She had come full circle; she looked up and said,

"Yes Mom, I did learn everything the hard way."

It dawned on her that while people who were not emotionally connected to Zach might look at him as the nice guy, who likes every one, who is helpful and kind. He has friends ranging from executives, doctors, police officers, all the way to down and out jobless alcoholics.

Each one seemed to have a purpose in his life, to serve him. His connection with executives made him appear important, legitimate and got him jobs. His doctor friends kindly provided free medical service and medication. His police officer friends made him appear above the law. His down and out jobless alcoholic friends seemed to do his dirty work; labor jobs. They were oblivious to their purpose; he was their friend. He says, "That's business."

Women are not only there for the obvious reason but he seemed to feel they were the 'weaker sex' and more readily conned. In addition, what woman does not admire a man who takes good care of his mother? Even she was being used. He seemed to use their emotions and egos against them. It appears to his friends he has the perfect life.

Because, he never stays long in one place, it would be difficult to figure him out. In relationships however, he cannot escape often enough. He must keep moving, but then again that depends on how much he can get if he stays.

If his victim has the potential to make him a lot of money, he does the first project free or next to it and, before he finishes that project, he gets her on the hook for the next and the next. This will continue until she figures him out or she runs out of money.

Desiree believed Zach and his wife were together so long, because they lived two separate lives. It was also the reason he would encourage Desiree to keep herself busy, "You need to find something to do," he would often say. He wanted her to keep busy so she would not look over her shoulder to see what he was doing. When she became suspicious, he would then leave clues for her to chase. If she would not keep busy on her own, he would lead her in another direction and that would keep her busy and, 'out of his business.'

He is trying something he has never tried before; he is in a relationship with the job. He always tried to keep that separate; he will "just see where it goes."

Printed in the United States
129320LV00005B/1-105/P